# WITH CHRIST
# IN THE SCHOOL
# OF OBEDIENCE

# ANDREW
# MURRAY

While this book is designed for
your personal enjoyment,
it is also intended for group study.
A Leader's Guide with Victor
Multiuse Transparency Masters
is available from your local bookstore
or from the publisher.

**VICTOR**

**BOOKS** a division of SP Publications, Inc.
WHEATON, ILLINOIS 60187

*Offices also in*
Whitby, Ontario, Canada
Amersham-on-the-Hill, Bucks, England

**The Classic Electives from Victor Books**

*Getting Things from God* by Charles A. Blanchard
*Inherit the Kingdom* by F.B. Meyer
*Kept for the Master's Use* by Frances R. Havergal
*With Christ in the School of Obedience* by Andrew Murray

Most Scripture quotations in this book are from the *King James Version* of the Bible. Others are from the *American Standard Version* (ASV).

Recommended Dewey Decimal Classification: 248.4
Suggested Subject Heading: CHRISTIAN LIFE

Library of Congress Catalog Card Number: 85-62718
ISBN: 0-89693-281-8

VICTOR BOOKS
A division of SP Publications, Inc.
Wheaton, Illinois 60187

# CONTENTS

# PREFACE

These addresses on obedience are issued with the very fervent prayer that it may please our gracious Father to use them for the instruction and strengthening of the young men and women on whose obedience and devotion so much depends for the church and the world. The God of all grace bless them abundantly!

It often happens after a conference, or even after writing a book, that it is as if one only then begins to see the meaning and importance of the truth with which one has been occupied. So I do indeed feel as if I had utterly failed in grasping or expounding the spiritual character, the altogether indispensable necessity, the divine and actual possibility, the inconceivable blessedness of a life of true and entire obedience to our Father in heaven. Let me, therefore, just in a few sentences gather up the main points which have come home to me with special power, and ask every reader at starting to take note of them as some of the chief lessons to be learned in Christ's school of obedience.

The Father in heaven asks and requires and actually expects that every child of His yield Him wholehearted and entire obedience day by day and all the day.

To enable His child to do this, He has made a most abundant and altogether sufficient provision in the promise of the New Covenant, and in the gift of His Son and Spirit.

This provision can only be enjoyed, and these promises fulfilled, in the soul that gives itself up to a life in abiding communion with the three-one God, so that His presence and power work in it all the day.

The very entrance into this life demands the vow of absolute obedience, or the surrender of the whole being, to be, think, speak, and do every moment, nothing but what is according to the will of God, and well-pleasing to Him.

If these things be indeed true, it is not enough to assent to them; we need the Holy Spirit to give us such a vision of their glory and divine power, and the demand they make on our immediate and unconditional submission, that there may be no rest till we accept all that God is willing to do for us.

Let us all pray that God may, by the light of His Spirit, so show His loving and almighty will concerning us, that it may be impossible for us to be disobedient to the heavenly vision.

ANDREW MURRAY    1885

# CHAPTER ONE

# OBEDIENCE: ITS PLACE
# IN HOLY SCRIPTURE

"Have not I commanded thee?" (Joshua 1:9)

I n studying a Bible word or a truth of the Christian life, it is helpful to also study its place in Scripture. As we see where and how often and in what connections it is found, its relative importance may be understood as well as its bearing on the whole of revelation. Let me try in the first chapter to prepare the way for the study of what obedience is by showing you where to go in God's Word to find the mind of God concerning it.

### Take Scripture as a Whole

We begin with paradise. In Genesis 2:16 we read: "And the Lord God commanded the man, saying." And later, "Hast thou eaten of the tree, whereof I commanded thee that thou shouldest not eat?" (3:11)

Note how obedience to the command is the one virtue

of paradise, the one condition of man's abiding there, the one thing his Creator asks of him. Nothing is said of faith or humility or love; obedience includes all. The demand for obedience as the one thing that is to decide his destiny is as supreme as the claim and authority of God. In the life of man, to obey is the one thing needful.

Turn now from the beginning to the close of the Bible. In its last chapter you read, "Blessed are they that do His commandments, that they may have a right to the tree of life" (Rev. 22:14). The same thoughts also occur earlier in Revelation, where we read of the seed of the woman "that keep the commandments of God, and hold the testimony of Jesus" (12:17, ASV) and of the patience of the saints, "Here . . . [are] they that keep the commandments of God, and the faith of Jesus" (14:12, ASV).

From beginning to end, from paradise lost to paradise regained, the law is unchangeable; it is only obedience that gives access to the tree of life and the favor of God.

And if you ask how the change was effected out of the disobedience at the beginning that closed the way to the tree of life, to the obedience at the end that again gained entrance to it, turn to that which stands midway between the beginning and the end: the Cross of Christ. Read a passage like Romans 5:19 (ASV), "Through the obedience of the One shall the many be made righteous"; or Philippians 2:8-9, "He became obedient unto death. . . . Wherefore God also hath highly exalted Him"; or Hebrews 5:8-9, "He learned obedience . . . and . . . became the author of eternal salvation unto all them that obey Him," and you see how the whole redemption of Christ consists in restoring obedience to its place. The beauty of His salvation

8

consists in this: that He brings us back to the life of obedience, through which alone the creature can give the Creator the glory due to Him, or receive the glory of which his Creator desires to make him partaker.

Paradise, Calvary, heaven, all proclaim with one voice: "Child of God, the first and the last thing thy God asks of thee is simple, universal, unchanging obedience."

## Old Testament Examples

Let us especially notice in the Old Testament how, with any new beginning in the history of God's kingdom, obedience always comes into special prominence.

● Take Noah, the new father of the human race, and you will find four times written, "According to all that God commanded him [Noah], so did he" (Gen. 6:22; cf. 7:5, 9, 16).

It is the man who does what God commands to whom God can entrust His work, whom God can use to be a savior of men.

● Think of Abraham, the father of the chosen race. "By faith Abraham . . . obeyed" (Heb. 11:8).

When he had been forty years in this school of faith-obedience, God came to perfect his faith and to crown it with His fullest blessing. Nothing could fit him for this but a crowning act of obedience. When he had bound his son on the altar, God came and said, "By Myself have I sworn . . . in blessing I will bless thee, and in multiplying I will multiply thy seed . . . in thy seed shall all nations of the earth be blessed; because thou hast obeyed My voice" (Gen. 22:16-18).

And to Isaac the Lord said, "I will perform the oath

which I swore unto Abraham . . . because that Abraham obeyed My voice" (26:3, 5).

Oh, when shall we learn how unspeakably pleasing obedience is in God's sight, and how unspeakable is the reward He bestows upon it! The way to be a blessing to the world is to be men of obedience, known by God and the world by this one mark: a will utterly given up to God's will. Let all who profess to walk in Abraham's footsteps walk thusly.

● Go on to Moses. At Sinai, God gave him the message to the people, "If ye will obey My voice . . . ye shall be a peculiar treasure unto Me above all people" (Ex. 19:5).

In the very nature of things it cannot be otherwise. God's holy will is His glory and perfection; it is only by an entrance into His will, by obedience, that it is possible to be His people.

● Take the building of the sanctuary in which God was to dwell. In the last three chapters of Exodus you have part or all of the expression nineteen times, "According to all the Lord commanded Moses, so did he." And then, "The glory of the Lord filled the tabernacle" (40:34). Just so, again in Leviticus 8—9, you have, with reference to the consecration of the priests and the tabernacle, the same expression twelve times. And then, "The glory of the Lord appeared unto all the people. And there came a fire out from before the Lord, and consumed . . . the burnt offering" (Lev. 9:23-24).

Words cannot make it plainer that it is amid what the obedience of His people has created that God delights to dwell, that it is the obedient He crowns with His favor and presence.

● After forty years of wandering in the wilderness and its terrible revelation of the fruit of disobedience, there was again a new beginning when the people were about to enter Canaan. Read Deuteronomy, with all Moses spoke in sight of the land, and you will find there is no book of the Bible which uses the word *obey* so frequently or speaks so much of the blessing obedience will assuredly bring. The whole is summed up in the words, "I set before you . . . a blessing, if ye obey . . . and a curse, if ye will not obey" (Deut. 11:26-28).

Yes, "a blessing, if ye obey"! That is the keynote of the blessed life. Canaan, just like paradise and heaven, can be the place of blessing *if* it is the place of obedience. Would to God we might take it in! But do beware of praying only for a blessing. Let us take care of the obedience; God will take care of the blessing. Let our one thought as Christians be, "How can I obey and please my God perfectly?"

● The next new beginning we have is in the appointment of kings in Israel. In the story of Saul we have the most solemn warning as to the need of exact and entire obedience in a man whom God is to trust as ruler of His people. Samuel had commanded Saul to wait seven days for him to come and sacrifice and to show him what to do (1 Sam. 10:8). When Samuel delayed, Saul took it upon himself to offer the sacrifice (13:8-14).

When Samuel came, he said: "Thou hast not kept the commandment of the Lord thy God, which He commanded thee . . . thy kingdom shall not continue . . . because thou hast not kept that which the Lord commanded thee" (vv. 13-14).

God will not honor the man who is not obedient.

Saul had a second opportunity given him to show what was in his heart. Commanded to execute God's judgment against Amalek, Saul gathered an army of 200,000 men, undertook the journey into the wilderness, and destroyed the Amalekites. But while God had commanded him to "utterly destroy all . . . and spare them not" (15:3), he spared the best of the cattle and Agag the king.

Then God spoke to Samuel, "It repenteth Me that I have set up Saul to be king: for he . . . hath not performed My commandments" (v. 11).

When Samuel at last came to Saul at Gilgal, Saul twice boasted, "I have performed the commandment of the Lord" (v. 13); "I have obeyed the voice of the Lord" (v. 20).

And so he had, as many would think. But his obedience had not been entire. God claims exact, full obedience. God had said, "Utterly destroy all! Spare not!" This he had not done. He had spared the best sheep for a sacrifice unto the Lord. And Samuel said, "To obey is better than [any] sacrifice. . . . Because thou hast rejected the word of the Lord, He hath also rejected thee" (vv. 22-23).

That is a sad type of so much obedience which in part performs God's commandment and yet is not the obedience God asks! God says of all sin and all disobedience: "Utterly destroy all! Spare not!" May God reveal to us whether we are indeed seeking utterly to destroy all and to spare nothing that is not in perfect harmony with His will. It is only a wholehearted obedience, down to the minutest details, that can satisfy God. Let nothing less satisfy you, lest while you say, "I have obeyed," God says, "Thou hast rejected the word of the Lord."

● Just one word more from the Old Testament. Next to Deuteronomy, Jeremiah is the book most full of the word *obey*, though, alas, mostly in connection with the complaint that the people had not obeyed. God sums up all His dealings with the Israelites in the one word: "I spoke not unto your fathers . . . concerning . . . sacrifices: but this thing commanded I them, saying, 'Obey My voice, and I will be your God' " (Jer. 7:22-23).

Would to God that we could learn that all that He speaks of sacrifices, even of the sacrifice of His beloved Son, is subordinate to the one thing: to have His creatures restored to full obedience. Into all the inconceivable meaning of the word, "I will be your God," there is no gateway but this: "Obey My voice."

### New Testament Examples

In the New Testament we think at once of our blessed Lord and the prominence He gives to obedience as the one thing for which He had come into the world. He who entered it with His "Lo, I come to do Thy will, O God" (Heb. 10:9), ever confessed to men, "I seek not Mine own will, but the will of the Father [who] hath sent Me" (John 5:30).

Of all He did and of all He suffered, even to the death, He said, "This commandment have I received of My Father" (10:18).

● If we turn to our Lord Jesus' teaching, we find everywhere that the obedience He rendered is what He claims from everyone who would be His disciple.

During His whole ministry, from beginning to end, obedience is the very essence of salvation. In the Sermon on the Mount He began with it. No one could enter the kingdom "but he that doeth the will of My Father which is in heaven" (Matt. 7:21). And in the farewell discourse, how wonderfully He reveals the spiritual character of true obedience as it is born of love and inspired by it, and as it also opens the way into the love of God. Do take into your heart the wonderful words, "If ye love Me, ye will keep My commandments. And . . . the Father . . . shall give you . . . the Spirit. He that hath My commandments, and keepeth them, he it is that loveth Me: and he . . . shall be loved of My Father, and I will love him, and will manifest Myself unto him. If a man love Me, he will keep My word: and My Father will love him, and We will come unto him, and make Our abode with him" (John 14:15-17, 21, 23, ASV).

No words could express more simply or more powerfully the inconceivably glorious place Christ gives to obedience, with its twofold possibility: (1) as only possible to a loving heart, (2) as making possible all that God has to give of His Holy Spirit, of His wonderful love, of His indwelling in Christ Jesus. I know of no passage in Scripture that gives a higher revelation of the spiritual life, or the power of loving obedience as its one condition. Let us pray and ask God very earnestly that by His Holy Spirit its light may transfigure our daily obedience with its heavenly glory.

See how all this is confirmed in John 15. How well we know the Parable of the Vine! How often and how earnestly we have asked how to be able to abide continually in Christ! We have thought of more study of the Word, more faith, more prayer, more communion with God, and we have overlooked the simple truth that Jesus teaches so clearly, "If ye keep My commandments, ye shall abide in My love," with its divine sanction: "Even as I kept My Father's commandments, and abide in His love" (v. 10).

For Him as for us, the only way under heaven to abide in divine love is to keep the commandments. Do let me ask: "Have you known it, have you heard it preached, have you believed it and proved it true in your experience that obedience on earth is the key to a place in God's love in heaven?" Unless there be some correspondence between God's wholehearted love in heaven and our wholehearted, loving obedience on earth, Christ cannot manifest Himself to us, God cannot abide in us, and we cannot abide in His love.

● If we go on from our Lord Jesus to His apostles, we find in Acts two words of Peter's which show how our Lord's teaching had entered into him. In the one, "The Holy Ghost, whom God hath given to them that obey Him" (Acts 5:32), he proves how he knew what had been the preparation for Pentecost: the surrender to Christ. In the other, "We must obey God rather than man" (v. 29, ASV), we have the manward side. Obedience is to be unto death; nothing on earth dare or can hinder it in the man who has given himself to God.

● In Paul's Epistle to the Romans, we have in the opening and closing verses the expression, "the obedience of faith among all the nations" (1:5, ASV; cf. 16:26), as that for which he was made an apostle. He speaks of what God had wrought "to make the Gentiles obedient" (15:18). He teaches that, as the obedience of Christ makes us righteous, we become the servants of obedience unto righteousness. As disobedience in Adam and in us was the one thing that brought death, so obedience, in Christ and in us, is the one thing that the Gospel makes known as the way of restoration to God and His favor.

● James warns us not to be hearers of the Word only but doers, and expounds how Abraham was justified, and his faith perfected by his works.

● In Peter's first epistle we have only to look at the first chapter to see the place obedience has in his system. In verse 2 he speaks to the "elect . . . through sanctification of the Spirit, unto obedience and sprinkling of the blood of Jesus Christ," and so points us to obedience as the eternal purpose of the Father, as the great object of the work of the Spirit, and a chief part of the salvation of Christ. He writes, "As children of obedience" (v. 14, ASV), born of it, marked by it, subject to it, "be ye holy in all manner of conversation" (v. 15). Obedience is the very starting point of true holiness. In verse 22 (ASV) we read, "Seeing ye have purified your souls in your obedience to the truth." The whole acceptance of the truth of God was not merely a matter of intellectual assent or strong emotion; it was a subjection of the life to the dominion of His truth. The Christian life was in the first place obedience.

● We know how strong the Apostle John's statements are. "He that saith, 'I know Him,' and keepeth not His commandments, is a liar" (1 John 2:4). Obedience is the one certificate of Christian character. "Let us . . . love . . . in deed and in truth . . . hereby we . . . shall assure our hearts before Him. . . . And whatsoever we ask, we receive of Him, because we keep His commandments, and do those things that are pleasing in His sight"

16

(3:18-22). Obedience is the secret of a good conscience and of the confidence that God hears us. "This is the love of God, that we keep His commandments" (5:3). The obedience that keeps His commandments is the garment in which the hidden, invisible love reveals itself, and whereby it is known.

Such is the place obedience has in Holy Scripture, in the mind of God, in the hearts of His servants. We may well ask, "Does it take that place in my heart and life? Have I indeed given obedience that supreme place of authority over me that God means it to have, as the inspiration of every action and of every approach to Him?" If we yield ourselves to the searching of God's Spirit, we may find that we never gave it its true proportion in our scheme of life, and that this lack is the cause of all our failure in prayer and in work. We may see that the deeper blessings of God's grace and the full enjoyment of God's love and nearness have been beyond our reach simply because obedience was never made what God would have it be: the starting point and the goal of our Christian lives.

Let this, our first study, waken in us an earnest desire to know God's will fully concerning this truth. Let us unite in praying that the Holy Spirit may show us how defective the Christian's life is where obedience does not rule all, how that life can be exchanged for one of full surrender to absolute obedience, and how sure it is that God in Christ will enable us to live it out.

# CHAPTER TWO

# THE OBEDIENCE OF CHRIST

"Through the obedience of the One shall the many
be made righteous." (Romans 5:19, ASV)
"Know ye not, that . . . ye [are] . . . servants . . .
of obedience unto righteousness?" (Romans 6:16)

Through the obedience of
the One shall the many be made righteous. These words
tell us what we owe to Christ. As in Adam we were made
sinners, in Christ we are made righteous.

The words also tell us to what in Christ it is we owe our
righteousness. As Adam's disobedience made us sinners,
the obedience of Christ makes us righteous. To the obedience of Christ we owe everything.

Among the treasures of our inheritance in Christ this is
one of the richest. How many have never studied it, so as
to love it and delight in it and get the full blessing of it!
May God by His Holy Spirit reveal its glory and make us
partakers of its power.

You are familiar with the blessed truth of justification
by faith. In the section of the Epistle to the Romans
preceding our passage (3:21—5:11), Paul had taught that

19

its ever-blessed foundation was the atoning blood of Christ; that its way and condition were faith in the free grace of God who justifies the ungodly; and that its blessed fruits were the bestowment of the righteousness of Christ, with an immediate access into the favor of God, and the hope of glory. In our passage Paul now proceeds to unfold the deeper truth of the union with Christ by faith, in which justification has its root, and which makes it possible and right for God to accept us for His sake. Paul goes back to Adam and our union with him, with all the consequences that flowed from that union, to prove how reasonable, how perfectly natural (in the higher sense of the word) it is that those who receive Christ by faith, and are so united with Him, become partakers of His righteousness and His life. It is in this argument that he specially emphasizes the contrast between the disobedience of Adam, with the condemnation and death it brought, and the obedience of Christ, with the righteousness and life it brings. As we study the place of Christ's obedience in His work for our salvation and see in it the very root of our redemption, we shall know what place to give it in our hearts and lives.

### Adam's Race

"Through the one man's disobedience the many were made sinners" (Rom. 5:19, ASV). How was this?

There was a twofold connection between Adam and his descendants: the judicial and the vital. Through the judicial, the whole race, though yet unborn, came at once under the sentence of death. "Death reigned from Adam to Moses, even over them"—such as little children—"that had not sinned after the likeness of Adam's transgression" (v. 14, ASV).

This judicial relation was rooted in the vital connection. The sentence could not have come upon them if they had not been in Adam. And the vital again becomes the manifestation of the judicial; each child of Adam enters life under the power of sin and death. "Through the disobedience of the one, the many were constituted sinners," both by position subject to the curse of sin, and by nature subject to its power.

"Adam . . . is the figure of Him that was to come" (v. 14), and who is called the second Adam, the second Father of the race. Adam's disobedience in its effects is the exact similitude of what the obedience of Christ becomes to us. When a sinner believes in Christ, he is united to Him and is at once, by a judicial sentence, pronounced and accepted as righteous in God's sight. The judicial relationship is rooted in the vital. He has Christ's righteousness only by having Christ Himself and being in Him. Before he knows anything of what it is to be in Christ, he can know himself acquitted and accepted. But he is then led on to know the vital connection and to understand that as real and complete as was his participation in Adam's disobedience with the death as well as the sinful nature that followed on it, so is his participation in Christ's obedience, with both the righteousness and the obedient life and nature that come from it.

Let us see and understand this: through Adam's disobedience we are made sinners. The one thing God asked of Adam in paradise was obedience. The one thing by which a creature can glorify God, or enjoy His favor and blessing, is obedience. The one cause of the power sin has got in the world, and the ruin it has wrought, is disobedience. The whole curse of sin on us is owing to disobedience imputed to us. The whole power of sin working in us is nothing but this: that as we receive Adam's nature, we inherit his disobedience, we are born "the children of disobedience."

## The Second Adam

It is evident that the one work Christ was needed for was to remove Adam's disobedience—its curse, its dominion, its evil nature and workings. Disobedience was the root of all sin and misery. The first object of His salvation was to cut away the evil root and to restore man to his original destiny: a life in obedience to his God.

How did Christ do this?

First of all, by coming as the second Adam to undo what the first had done. Sin had made us believe that it was a humiliation always to be seeking to know and do God's will. Christ came to show us the nobility, the blessedness, the heavenliness of obedience. When God gave us the robe of creaturehood to wear, we knew not that its beauty, its unspotted purity, was obedience to God. Christ came and put on that robe that He might show us how to wear it, and how with it we could enter into the presence and glory of God. Christ came to overcome and so bear away our disobedience and to replace it by His own obedience on us and in us. As universal, as mighty, as all-pervasive as was the disobedience of Adam, yea, far more so was to be the power of the obedience of Christ.

The object of Christ's life of obedience was threefold:

(1) *As an example* to show us what true obedience is.
(2) *As our surety* by His obedience to fulfill all righteousness for us. (3) *As our head* to prepare a new and obedient
nature to impart to us.

He also died to show us that His obedience means a
readiness to obey to the uttermost, to die for God; that it
means the vicarious endurance and atonement of the guilt
of our disobedience; that it means a death to sin as an
entrance to the life of God for Him and for us.

Judicially, by the obedience of Christ we are made
righteous. Just as we were made sinners by Adam's disobedience, we are at once and completely justified and
delivered from the power of sin and death; we stand
before God as righteous men. Vitally—for the judicial and
the vital are as inseparable as in the case of Adam—we are
made one with Christ in His death and resurrection so
that we are as truly dead to sin and alive to God as He is.
And the life we receive in Him is no other than a life of
obedience.

Let every one of us who desires obedience consider
well: it is the obedience of Christ that is the secret of the
righteousness and salvation we find in Him. The obedience is the very essence of that righteousness; obedience
is salvation. His obedience, first of all to be accepted, and
trusted, and rejoiced in, as covering and swallowing up
and making an end of our disobedience, is the one unchanging, never-to-be-forsaken ground of our acceptance.
And then, His obedience—just as Adam's disobedience
was the power that ruled our lives, the power of death in
us—becomes the life power of the new nature in us. Then
we understand why Paul in this passage so closely links

the righteousness and the life. "If, by the trespass of one, death reigned through the one: much more shall they that receive the abundance of grace and of the gift of righteousness reign in life through the One" (v. 17, ASV), even here on earth. "The free gift came unto all men to justification of life" (v. 18).

The more carefully we trace the parallel between the first and second Adam and see how in the former the death and disobedience reigned in his seed equally with himself, and how both were equally transmitted through union with him, the more will the conviction be forced upon us that the obedience of Christ is equally to be ours, not only by imputation, but by personal possession. It is so inseparable from Him that to receive Him and His life is to receive His obedience. When we receive the righteousness which God offers us so freely, it at once points us to the obedience out of which it was born, with which it is inseparably one, in which alone it can live and flourish.

See how this connection comes out in Romans 6. After having spoken of our life union to Christ, Paul for the first time in the epistle gives an injunction, "Let not sin therefore reign . . . but present yourselves unto God" (6:12-13, ASV); and then he immediately proceeds to teach how this means nothing but obedience: "Know ye not, that . . . ye [are] . . . servants . . . of sin unto death, or of obedience unto righteousness?" (v. 16)

### Practical Obedience

Your relation to obedience is a practical one; you have been delivered from disobedience (Adam's and your

24

own), and now have become a servant of obedience, and that "unto righteousness." Christ's obedience was unto righteousness, the righteousness which is God's gift to you. Your subjection to obedience is the one way in which your relation to God and to righteousness can be maintained. Christ's obedience unto righteousness is the only beginning of life for you; your obedience unto righteousness, its only continuance. There is but one law for the head and the members. As surely as it was disobedience and death with Adam and his seed, it is obedience and life with Christ and His seed. The one bond of union, the one mark of likeness, between Adam and his seed was disobedience. The one bond of union between Christ and His seed, the one mark of resemblance, is obedience.

Obedience alone made Christ the object of the Father's love (John 10:17-18) and our Redeemer, and obedience alone can lead us in the way to dwell in that love (14:21, 23) and enjoy that redemption.

"Through the obedience of the One shall the many be made righteous" (Rom. 5:19, ASV). Everything depends on our knowledge of and participation in the obedience as the gateway and path to the full enjoyment of the righteousness. At conversion the righteousness is given to faith, once for all, completely and forever, with but little or no knowledge of the obedience. But as the righteousness is indeed believed in and submitted to, and its full dominion over us as "servants of righteousness" sought after, it will open to us its blessed nature, as born out of obedience, and therefore ever leading us back to its divine origin. The truer our hold of the righteousness of Christ in the power of the Spirit, the more intense will be our desire to share in the obedience out of which it sprang.

## "I Come to Do Thy Will"

In this light let us study the obedience of Christ that, like Him, we may live as servants of obedience unto righteousness.

*In Christ this obedience was a life principle.* Obedience with Him did not mean a single act of obedience now and then, not even a series of acts, but the spirit of His whole life. "I came . . . not to do Mine own will" (John 6:38). "Lo, I come to do Thy will, O God" (Heb. 10:9). He had come into the world for one purpose. He only lived to carry out God's will. The one supreme, all-controlling power of His life was obedience.

He is willing to make it so in us. This was what He promised when He said, "Whosoever shall do the will of My Father which is in heaven, the same is My brother, and sister, and mother" (Matt. 12:50).

The link in a family is a common life shared by all and a family likeness. The bond between Christ and us is that He and we together do the will of God.

*In Christ this obedience was a joy.* "I delight to do Thy will, O my God" (Ps. 40:8). "My meat is to do the will of Him that sent Me" (John 4:34).

Our food is refreshment and invigoration. The healthy man eats his bread with gladness. But food is more than enjoyment; it is the one necessity of life. And so, doing the will of God was the food that Christ hungered after and without which He could not live, the one thing that satisfied His hunger, the one thing that refreshed and strengthened Him and made Him glad.

It was something of this that David meant when he spoke of God's words being "sweeter also than honey and the honeycomb" (Ps. 19:10). As this is understood and accepted, obedience will become more natural to us and necessary to us, and more refreshing than our daily food.

*In Christ this obedience led to a waiting on God's will.* God did not reveal all His will to Christ at once, but day by day, acccording to the circumstances of the hour. In His life of obedience there were growth and progress; the most difficult lesson came last. Each act of obedience fitted Him for the new discovery of the Father's further command.

It is as obedience becomes the passion of our lives that the ears will be opened by God's Spirit to wait for His teaching (40:6), and we will be content with nothing less than a divine guidance into the divine will for us.

*In Christ this obedience was unto death.* When He said, "I came . . . not to do Mine own will, but the will of Him that sent Me" (John 6:38), He was ready to go all lengths in denying His own will and doing the Father's. He meant it. "In nothing My will; at all costs God's will."

This is the obedience to which He invites and for which He empowers us. This wholehearted surrender to obedience in everything is the only true obedience; it is the only power that will avail to carry us through. Would to God that Christians could understand that nothing less than this is what brings the soul gladness and strength!

As long as there is a doubt about universal obedience, and with that a lurking sense of the possibility of failure, we lose the confidence that secures the victory. But when once we set God before us as really asking full obedience, and engaging to work it, and see that we dare offer Him nothing less, we give up ourselves to the working of the divine power which by the Holy Spirit can master our whole lives.

*In Christ this obedience sprang from the deepest humility.* "Have this mind in you, which was also in Christ Jesus: who . . . emptied Himself, taking the form of a servant . . . and . . . humbled Himself, becoming obedient even unto death" (Phil. 2:5-8, ASV).

It is the man who is willing for entire self-emptying, is willing to be and live as the servant, "a servant of obedience," is willing to be humbled very low before God and man, to whom the obedience of Jesus will unfold its heavenly beauty and its constraining power. There may be a strong will that secretly trusts in self, that strives for the obedience and fails. It is as we sink low before God in humility, meekness, patience, and entire resignation to His will and are willing to bow in absolute helplessness and dependence on Him, as we turn away wholly from self, that it will be revealed to us how it is the one duty and blessing of a creature to obey this glorious God!

*In Christ this obedience was of faith,* in entire dependence upon God's strength. "I can of Mine own self do nothing" (John 5:30). "The Father that dwelleth in Me, He doeth the works" (14:10).

The Son's unreserved surrender to the Father's will was met by the Father's unceasing and unreserved bestowment of His power working in Him.

It will be even so with us. If we learn that giving up our will to God is ever the measure of His giving His power in us, we shall see that a surrender to full obedience is nothing but a full faith that God will work all in us.

God's promises of the New Covenant all rest on this: "The Lord thy God will circumcise thine heart . . . to love the Lord thy God with all thine heart . . . and thou shalt return and obey . . . the Lord thy God" (Deut. 30:6-9). "I will put My Spirit within you, and cause you to walk in My statutes, and ye shall keep My judgments" (Ezek. 36:27).

Let us, like the Son, believe that God works all in us, and we shall have the courage to yield ourselves to an unreserved obedience, an obedience unto death. Such yielding will become the entrance into the blessed experience of conformity to the Son of God in His doing the Father's will because He counted on the Father's power. Let us give our all to God. He will work His all in us.

It is in the obedience of the One that the obedience of the many has its root, its life, its security. Let us turn as never before and gaze upon and study and believe in Christ as the obedient One. Let this be the Christ we receive and love and seek to be made comformable to. As His righteousness is our one hope, let His obedience be our one desire. Let our faith in Him prove its sincerity and its confidence in God's supernatural power working in us by accepting Christ, the obedient One, as our very life, as the Christ who dwells in us.

# CHAPTER THREE

# THE SECRET
# OF TRUE OBEDIENCE

"He . . . learned . . . obedience." (Hebrews 5:8)

The secret of true obedience, I believe, is a clear and close personal relationship to God. All our attempts to achieve full obedience will be failures until we enter His abiding fellowship. It is God's holy presence consciously abiding with us that keeps us from disobeying Him.

Defective obedience is always the result of a defective life. We need a different life, a life so entirely under the power of God that obedience will be its natural outcome. The defective life, the life of broken and irregular fellowship with God, must be healed to make way for a full and healthy life; then full obedience will become possible. The secret of true obedience is the return to close and continual fellowship with God.

According to the writer to the Hebrews, Jesus Christ learned obedience (Heb. 5:8). How did He do this and why was it necessary? "He . . . learned . . . obedience by the things which He suffered; and . . . became the author of eternal salvation unto all them that obey Him" (vv. 5-9).

Suffering is unnatural to us and therefore calls for the surrender of our wills. Christ needed suffering that in it He might learn to obey and give up His will to the Father at any cost. He needed to learn obedience that as our great High Priest He might be made perfect. He learned obedience; He became obedient unto death that He might become the author of our salvation. He became the author of salvation through obedience that He might save those "who obey Him."

As obedience was with Him absolutely necessary to procure salvation, it is with us absolutely necessary to inherit it. The very essence of salvation is obedience to God. Christ as the obedient One saves us as His obedient ones. Whether in His suffering on earth or in His glory in heaven, whether in Himself or in us, obedience is what the heart of Christ is set upon.

On earth Christ was a student in the school of obedience; from heaven He teaches it to His disciples here on earth. In a world where disobedience reigns unto death, the restoration of obedience is in Christ's hands. As in His own life, so in us, He has undertaken to maintain it. He teaches and works it in us.

Let us now examine what and how He teaches. It may be we shall see how little we have given of ourselves to be pupils in this school, where obedience alone is to be learned. When we think of an ordinary school, the principal things we often ask about are: (1) the teacher, (2) the textbooks, and (3) the pupils. Let us see what each of these is in Christ's school of obedience.

### The Teacher

"He . . . learned . . . obedience." And now that He teaches it, He does so first and foremost by unfolding the secret of His own obedience to the Father.

I have said that the power of true obedience is to be found in a clear personal relationship to God. So it was with our Lord Jesus. Of all His teaching He said, "I have not spoken of Myself; but the Father which sent Me . . . gave Me a commandment, what I should say, and what I should speak. And I know that His commandment is life everlasting: whatsoever I speak therefore, even as the Father said unto Me, so I speak" (John 12:49-50).

This does not mean that Christ received God's commandment in eternity as part of the Father's commission to Him on entering the world. No. Day by day, each moment as He taught and worked, He lived as man in continual communication with the Father and received the Father's instructions just as He needed them. Does He not say, "The Son can do nothing of Himself, but what He seeth the Father do. . . . For the Father . . . showeth Him all things that [He] doeth: and He will show Him greater works" (5:19-20); "As I hear, I judge" (v. 30); "I am not alone, but I and the Father that sent Me" (8:16); "The words that I speak . . . I speak not of Myself: but the Father that dwelleth in Me"? (14:10) It is everywhere a dependence upon a present fellowship and operation of God, a hearing and a seeing of what God speaks and does and shows.

Our Lord always spoke of His relation to the Father as the type and the promise of our relation to Him and to the Father through Him. With us as with Him, the life of continual obedience is impossible without continual fellowship and continual teaching. It is only when God comes into our lives, in a degree and a power which many never consider possible, when His presence as the eternal and ever-present One is believed and received, even as the Son believed and received it, that there can be any hope of a life in which every thought is brought into captivity to the obedience of Christ.

The fact that we must *continually* receive our orders and instructions from God Himself is implied in the words: "Obey My voice, and I will be your God" (Jer. 7:23).

The expression "obeying the commandments" is very seldom used in Scripture; it is almost always, "obeying Me," or "obeying [or, hearkening to] My voice." With an army commander, a schoolteacher, or a parent, it is not the code of laws, however clear and good, with its rewards or threats, that secures true obedience; it is the personal living influence, wakening love and enthusiasm. It is the joy of ever hearing the Father's voice that will give the joy and the strength of true obedience. It is the voice that gives power to obey the Word; the Word without the living voice does not avail.

How clearly this is illustrated by the contrast of what we see in the Israelites. The people had heard the voice of God on Sinai and were afraid. They asked Moses that God might no more speak to them. Let Moses receive the word of God and bring it to them. They only thought of the commands; they knew not that the only power to obey is in the presence of God and His voice speaking to us. And so with only Moses to speak to them, and the tables of stone, their whole history is one of disobedience because they were afraid of direct contact with God.

It is even so still. Many Christians find it so much easier to take their teaching from godly men than to wait upon God to receive it from Him. Their faith stands in the wisdom of men and not in the power of God.

The Lord Jesus, "who learned obedience" by every moment waiting to see and hear the Father, has a great lesson to teach us. It is only when, like Him, with Him, in and through Him, we walk with God moment by moment and hear His voice that we can possibly attempt to offer God the obedience He asks of us and promises to work in us.

Out of the depths of His own life and experience, Christ can give and teach us this. Pray earnestly that God may show you the folly of attempting to obey without the same strength Christ needed, may make you willing to give up everything for the Christlike joy of the Father's presence all the day.

### The Textbook

Christ's direct communication with the Father did not render Him independent of Holy Scripture. In the divine school of obedience there is but one textbook, whether for the elder Brother or the younger children. In learning obedience, Jesus used the same textbook as we have. Not only when He had to teach or to convince others did He appeal to the Word. He needed it and He used it for His own spiritual life and guidance.

From the beginning of His public life to its close Jesus lived by the Word of God. "It is written" was the sword of the Spirit with which He conquered Satan in the wilderness (Matt. 4:4, 7, 10). "The Spirit of the Lord is upon Me" (Luke 4:18); this word of Scripture was the consciousness with which He opened His preaching of the Gospel. "That the Scripture might be fulfilled" (John 17:12) was the light in which He accepted all suffering and even gave Himself to the death. After the Resurrection He expounded to the disciples "in all the Scriptures the things concerning Himself" (Luke 24:27).

In Scripture He had found God's plan and path marked out for Him. He gave Himself to fulfill it. It was in and with the use of God's Word that He received the Father's continual direct teaching.

In God's school of obedience the Bible is the only textbook. That shows us the disposition in which we are to come to the Bible: with the simple desire in it to find what is written concerning God's will, *and to do it.*

Scripture was not written to increase our knowledge but to guide our conduct "that the man of God may be perfect, thoroughly furnished unto all good works" (2 Tim. 3:17). "If any man will do His will, he shall know" (John 7:17). Learn from Christ to consider all there is in Scripture of the revelation of God, His love, and His counsel. The wisdom gained thereby helps to achieve God's great end: that the man of God may be fitted to do His will as it is done in heaven; that man may be restored to that perfect obedience on which God's heart is set and which alone is blessedness.

In God's school of obedience God's Word is the only

textbook. To apply that Word in His own life and conduct, to know when each different portion was to be taken up and carried out, Christ needed and received a divine teaching. It is He who speaks in Isaiah, "The Lord God . . . wakeneth morning by morning, He wakeneth Mine ear to hear as the learned. The Lord God hath opened Mine ear" (Isa. 50:4-5).

Even so does He who thus learned obedience teach it to us by giving us the Holy Spirit in our hearts as the divine interpreter of the Word. This is the great work of the indwelling Holy Spirit: to draw the Word we read and think upon into our hearts and make it quick and powerful there, so that God's living Word may work effectually in our will, our love, our whole being. It is because this is not understood that the Word has no power to work obedience.

Let me try and speak very plainly about this. We rejoice in increased attention given to Bible study, and in testimonies as to the interest awakened and benefit received. But let us not deceive ourselves. We may delight in studying the Bible; we may admire and be charmed with the views we get of God's truth. The thoughts suggested may make a deep impression and waken the most pleasing religious emotions, and yet the practical influence in making us holy or humble, loving, patient, ready either for service or suffering, may be very small. The one reason for this is that we do not receive the Word, as it is in very deed, as the Word of a living God who must Himself speak to us, and into us, if it is to exert its divine power.

The letter of the Word, however we study and delight in it, has no saving or sanctifying power. Human wisdom and human will, however strenuous their effort, cannot give, cannot command that power. The Holy Spirit is the mighty power of God. It is only as the Spirit teaches you, only as the Gospel is preached to you by man or by book, "with the Holy Ghost sent down from heaven" (1 Peter 1:12), that it will really give you, with every command, the strength to obey, and will work in you the very thing commanded.

With man, knowing and willing, knowing and doing, even willing and performing, are, for lack of power, often separate, and even at variance. Never in the Holy Spirit. He is at once the light and the might of God. All He is and does and gives has in it equally the truth and the power of God. When He shows you God's command, He always shows it to you as a possible and a certain thing, a divine life and gift prepared for you, which He who shows is able to impart.

Beloved Bible students, learn to believe that it is only when Christ through the Holy Spirit teaches you to understand and take the Word into your heart that He can really teach you to obey as He did. Every time you open your Bible, believe that just as surely as you listen to the divine, Spirit-breathed Word, so surely will our Father, in answer to the prayer of faith and docile waiting, give the Holy Spirit's living operation in your heart. Let all your Bible study be a thing of faith. Do not only try to believe the truths or promises you read. This may be in your own power. Before that, believe in the Holy Spirit, in His being in you, in God's working in you through Him. Take the Word into your heart in the quiet faith that He will enable you to love it and yield to it and keep it, and our blessed Lord Jesus will make the Book to you what it was to Him when He spoke of "the things [which are written] concerning Himself" (Luke 24:27). All Scripture will become the simple revelation of what God is going to do for you and in you and through you.

### The Pupil

We have seen how our Lord teaches us obedience by unfolding the secret of His learning it, in unceasing dependence on the Father. We have seen how He teaches us to use the sacred Book as He used it, as a divine revelation of what God has ordained for us, with the Holy Spirit to expound and enforce it. If we now consider the place the believer takes in the school of obedience as a pupil, we shall better understand what Christ the Son requires to do His work in us effectually.

In a faithful student several things make up his feelings toward a trusted teacher: he submits himself entirely to the teacher's leading; he places complete trust in him; he gives him just as much time and attention as is asked.

When we see and consent that Jesus Christ has a right to all this, He can teach us an obedience like His own.
● The true pupil, say of some great musician or painter, yields his master a wholehearted and unhesitating submission.

In practicing his scales or mixing the colors, in the slow and patient study of the elements of his art, he knows that it is wisdom simply and fully to obey.

It is this wholehearted surrender to His guidance, this implicit submission to His authority, which Christ asks. We come to Him asking Him to teach us the lost art of obeying God as He did. He asks us if we are ready to pay the price. It is entirely and utterly to deny self! It is to give up our will and our life to the death! It is to be ready to do whatever He says.

The only way of learning to do a thing is to do it. The only way of learning obedience from Christ is to give up your will to Him and to make the doing of His will the one desire and delight of your heart.

Unless you take the vow of absolute obedience as you enter this class of Christ's school, it will be impossible for you to make any progress.

● The true scholar of a great master finds it easy to render him this implicit obedience, simply because he trusts him. He gladly sacrifices his own wisdom and will to be guided by a higher.

We need this confidence in our Lord Jesus. He came from heaven to learn obedience that He might be able to teach it well. His obedience is the treasury out of which, not only the debt of our past obediences is paid, but out of which the grace for our present obedience is supplied. In His divine love and perfect human sympathy, in His divine power over our hearts and lives, He invites, He deserves, He wins our trust. It is by the power of a personal admiration and attachment to Himself, it is by the power of His divine love, in very deed shed into our hearts by the Holy Spirit and awakening within us a responsive love, that He awakens our confidence and communicates to us the true secret of success in His school. As absolutely as we have trusted Him as a Saviour to atone for our disobedience, so let us trust Him as a teacher to lead us out of it. Christ is our prophet or teacher. A heart that enthusiastically believes in His power and success as a teacher will, in the joy of that faith, find it possible and easy to obey. It is the presence of Christ with us all the day that will be the secret of true obedience.

● A scholar gives his master just as much of his attendance and attention as his master asks. The master fixes how much time must be devoted to personal fellowship and instruction.

Obedience to God is such a heavenly art, our nature is so utterly strange to it, and the path in which the Son Himself learned it was so slow and long that we must not wonder if it does not come at once. Nor must we wonder if it needs more time at the Master's feet in meditation and prayer, in waiting, dependence, and self-sacrifice than most believers are ready to give. But let us give it.

In Christ Jesus heavenly obedience has become human again, obedience has become our birthright and our life breath; let us cling to Him, let us believe and claim His abiding presence. With Jesus Christ who learned obedience as our Saviour, with Jesus Christ who teaches obedience as our Master, we can live lives of obedience. His obedience—we cannot study the lesson too earnestly—His obedience is our salvation; in Him, the living Christ, we find it and partake of it moment by moment.

Let us beseech God to show us how Christ and His obedience are actually to be our life every moment; that will then make us pupils who give Him all our hearts and all our time. And He will teach us to keep His commandments and abide in His love, even as He kept His Father's commandments and abides in His love.

41

# CHAPTER FOUR

# THE MORNING WATCH IN THE LIFE OF OBEDIENCE

"If the firstfruit is holy, so is the lump: and if the root is holy, so are the branches." (Romans 11:16, ASV)

How wonderful and blessed is the divine appointment of the first day of the week as a holy day of rest. Not (as some think) that we might have at least one day of rest and spiritual refreshment amid the weariness of life, but that this one holy day, at the opening of the week, might sanctify the whole, might help and fit us to carry God's holy presence into all the week and its work. With the firstfruit holy, the whole lump is holy; with the root holy, all the branches are holy too.

How gracious too the provision suggested by so many types and examples of the Old Testament, by which a morning hour at the opening of the day can enable us to secure a blessing for all its work and give us the assurance of power for victory over every temptation. How unspeakably gracious that in the morning hour the bond that unites us with God can be so firmly tied that during hours when we have to move amid the rush of men or duties and can scarcely think of God, the soul can be kept safe and pure; that the soul can so give itself away in the time of secret worship into His keeping, that temptation shall only help us unite it closer with Him. What cause for praise and joy that the morning watch can so each day renew and strengthen the surrender to Jesus and the faith in Him that the life of obedience cannot only be maintained in fresh vigor, but can indeed go on from strength to strength.

## The Motivational Principle

Think first of the motivational principle that will make us love and faithfully keep the morning watch. If we take it upon us simply as a duty and a necessary part of our religious life, it will very soon become a burden. Or, if the chief thought be our own happiness and safety, that will not supply the power to make it truly attractive. There is only one thing that will suffice: the desire for fellowship with God.

It is for fellowship we were created in God's likeness. It is that in which we hope to spend eternity. It is that alone which can fit us for a true and blessed life, either here or hereafter. To have more of God, to know Him better, to receive from Him the communication of His love and strength, to have our lives filled with His—it is for this He invites us to enter the inner chamber and shut the door.

It is in the closet, in the morning watch, that our spiritual life is both tested and strengthened. There is the battlefield where it is to be decided every day whether God is to have all, whether our lives are to be absolute obedience. If we truly conquer there, getting rid of ourselves into the hands of our Almighty Lord, the victory during the day is sure. It is there, in the inner chamber, that proof is to be given whether we really delight in God and make it our aim to love Him with our whole heart.

Let this, then, be our first lesson: the presence of God is the most important thing in our devotions. To meet God, to give ourselves into His holy will, to know that we are pleasing to Him, to have Him give us our orders and lay His hand upon us and bless us and say to us, "Go in this thy might" (Jud. 6:14)—it is when the soul learns that this is what is to be found in the morning watch, day by day, that we shall learn to long for it and delight in it.

### Reading the Bible

Part of the morning watch ought to be occupied with reading God's Word. With regard to this I have several points I wish to make.

● One is that unless we beware, the Word which is meant to point us toward God may actually intervene and hide Him from us.

The mind may be occupied and interested and delighted at what it finds, and yet, because this is more head knowledge than anything else, it may bring little good to us. If it does not lead us to wait on God, to glorify Him, to receive His grace and power for sweetening and sanctifying our lives, it becomes a hindrance instead of a help.

● Another lesson that cannot be repeated too often or pressed too urgently is that it is only by the teaching of the Holy Spirit that we can get at the real meaning of what

God means by His Word, and that the Word will really reach into our inner lives and work in us.

The Father in heaven, who gave us His Word with its divine mysteries and message, has given us His Holy Spirit within to explain and internally appropriate that Word. The Father wants us each time to ask that He teach us by His Spirit. He wants us to bow in a meek, teachable frame of mind and believe that the Spirit will, in the hidden depths of our hearts, make His Word live and work. He wants us to remember that the Spirit is given to us that we should be led by Him, should walk after Him, should have our whole lives under His rule, and that therefore He cannot teach us in the morning unless we honestly give up ourselves to His leading. But if we do this and patiently wait on Him, not to get new thoughts but to get the power of the Word in our hearts, we can count on His teaching.

Let your closet be the classroom, let your morning watch be the study hour, in which your relation of entire dependence on and submission to the Holy Spirit's teaching is proved to God.

• A third remark I want to make in confirmation of what was said previously is this: always study God's Word in the spirit of an unreserved surrender to obey.

You know how often Christ and His apostles, in their epistles, speak of hearing and not doing. If you accustom yourself to study the Bible without an earnest and very definite purpose to obey, you are getting hardened in disobedience.

Never read God's will concerning you without honestly giving up yourself to do it at once and asking grace to do so. God has given us His Word to tell us what He wants us to do and what grace He has provided to enable us to do it. How sad to think it a pious thing just to read that Word without any earnest effort to obey it! May God keep us from this terrible sin!

Let us make it a sacred habit to say to God, "Lord, whatever I know to be Thy will, I will at once obey." Always read with a heart yielded up in willing obedience.

● One more remark. I have here spoken of such commands as we already know, and as are easily understood. But, remember, there are a great many commands to which your attention may never have been directed, or others of which the application is so wide and unceasing that you have not taken it in. Read God's Word with a deep desire to know all His will. If there are things which appear difficult, commands which look too high or for which you need a divine guidance to tell you how to carry them out—and there are many such—let them drive you to seek a divine teaching. It is not the text that is easiest and most encouraging that brings the most blessing, but the text, whether easy or difficult, which throws you most upon God. God would have you "filled with the knowledge of His will in all wisdom and spiritual understanding" (Col. 1:9); it is in the closet this wonderful work is to be done. Do remember, it is only when you know that God is telling you to do a thing that you feel sure He gives the strength to do it. It is only as we are willing to know all God's will that He will from time to time reveal more of it to us and that we will be able to do it all.

What a power the morning watch may be in the life of one who makes a determined resolve to meet God there, to renew the surrender to absolute obedience, humbly and patiently to wait on the Holy Spirit to be taught all God's will, and to receive the assurance that every promise given him in the Word will infallibly be made true! He that thus prays for himself will become a true intercessor for others.

### Prayer

It is in the light of these thoughts I want now to say a few words on what prayer is to be in the morning watch.
● First of all, see that you secure the presence of God. Do not be content with anything less than seeing the face of God, having the assurance that He is looking on you in love, and listening and working in you.

If our daily lives are to be full of God, how much more the morning hour, where the life of the day alone can have God's seal stamped on it. In our religion we want nothing so much as more of God—His love, His will, His holiness, His Spirit living in us, His power working in us for men. Under heaven there is no way of getting this but by close personal communion. And there is no time so good for securing and practicing it as the morning watch.

The superficiality and feebleness of our religion and religious work all come from having so little real contact with God. If it be true that God alone is the foundation of all love and good and happiness, and that to have as much as possible of His presence and His fellowship, of His will and His service, is our trust and highest happiness, surely then to meet Him alone in the morning watch ought to be our first care.

To have God appear to them and speak to them was

with all the Old Testament saints the secret of their obedience and their strength. Do give God time in secret so to reveal Himself that your soul may call the name of the place Peniel, "for I have seen God face to face" (Gen. 32:30).

● My next thought is: let the renewal of your surrender to absolute obedience for that day be a chief part of your morning sacrifice.

Let any confession of sin be very definite, a plucking out and cutting off of everything that has grieved God. Let any prayer for grace for a holy walk be as definite, an asking and accepting in faith of the very grace and strength you are specially in need of. Let your outlook on the day you are entering be a very determined resolve that obedience to God shall be its controlling principle.

There is no surer way, indeed there is no other possible way, of getting into God's love and blessing in prayer than by getting into His will. In prayer, give up yourself most absolutely to the blessed will of God; this will avail more than much asking. Beseech God to show you this great mercy that He allows you that He will enable you to enter into His will and abide there. That will make knowing and doing His will in your life a blessed certainty. Let your prayer indeed be a "morning sacrifice," a placing of yourself as a whole burnt offering on the altar of the Lord.

The measure of surrender to full obedience will be the measure of confidence toward God.

● Then remember that true prayer and fellowship with God cannot be all from one side.

We need to be still, to wait and hear God's response. This is the office of the Holy Spirit, to be the voice of God to us. In the hidden depths of the heart, He can give a secret but most certain assurance that we are heard, that we are well-pleasing, that the Father engages to do for us what we have asked. What we need to hear the voice, to receive this assurance, is the quiet stillness that waits on God, the quiet faith that trusts in God, the quiet heart that bows in nothingness and humility before God and allows Him to be all in all.

It is when God is waited on to take His part in our prayer that the confidence will come to us that we receive what we ask, that our surrender of ourselves in the sacrifice of obedience is accepted, and that therefore we can count on the Holy Spirit to guide us into all the will of God as He means us to know and do it.

What glory would come to us in the morning watch, and through it into our daily lives, if it were thus made an hour spent with the Triune God, for the Father, through the Son and the Spirit, to take conscious possession of us for the day. How little need there then would be to urge and plead with God's children to watch the morning watch!

● And now comes the last and the best of all. Let your prayer be intercessional on behalf of others. In the obedience of our Lord Jesus, as in all His fellowship with the Father, the essential element was that it was all for others. This Spirit flows through every member of the body of Christ; the more we know it and yield to it, the more will our lives be what God would make them. The highest form of prayer is intercession. The chief object for which God chose Abraham and Israel and us was to make us a blessing to the world. We are a royal priesthood, a priestly people. As long as prayer is only a means of personal improvement and happiness, we cannot know its full power. Let intercession be a real longing for the souls of those around us, a real bearing of the burden of their sin and need, a real pleading for the extension of God's kingdom, real labor in prayer for definite purposes to be realized. Let such intercession be what the morning watch is consecrated to, and see what new interest and attraction it will have.

Intercession! Oh, to realize what it means! To take the name and the righteousness and the worthiness of Christ, to put them on, and in them to appear before God! "In Christ's stead" (2 Cor. 5:20), now that He is no longer in the world, to beseech God by name for the individual men and needs where His grace can do its work! In the faith of our own acceptance and of the anointing with the Spirit to fit us for the work, to know that our prayer can avail to "save a soul from death" (James 5:20), can bring down and dispense the blessing of heaven on earth! To think that in the hour of the morning watch this work can be renewed and carried on day by day, each inner chamber maintaining its own separate communication with heaven, and helping together in bringing down its share of the blessing.

It is in intercession, more than in the zeal that works in its own strength with little prayer, that the highest type of piety, the true Christlikeness, is cultivated. It is in intercession that a believer rises to his true nobility in the power of imparting life and blessing. It is to intercession we must look for any large increase of the power of God in the church and its work for men.

One word in conclusion. Turn back and think now again about the intimate and vital connection between obedience and the morning watch.

Without obedience there cannot be the spiritual power to enter into the knowledge of God's Word and will. Without obedience there cannot be the confidence, the boldness, the liberty that knows that it is heard. Obedience is fellowship with God in His will; without it there is not the capacity for seeing and claiming and holding the blessings He has for us.

And so, on the other side, without very definite living communication with God in the morning watch, the life of obedience cannot possibly be maintained. It is there that the vow of obedience can every morning be renewed in power and confirmed from above. It is there that the presence and fellowship can be secured which make obedience possible. It is there that in the obedience of the One, and in the union with Himself, the strength is received for all that God can ask. It is there that the spiritual understanding of God's will, which leads to a walk worthy of the Lord, is received.

God has called His children to live wonderful, heavenly, altogether supernatural lives. Let the morning watch each day be to you as the open gate of heaven through which its light and power stream in on your waiting heart, and from which you go out to walk with God all the day.

# CHAPTER FIVE

# THE ENTRANCE TO THE LIFE OF FULL OBEDIENCE

"Obedient unto death." (Philippians 2:8)

**A**fter all that has been said on the life of obedience, I purpose to consider the entrance into that life.

You might think it a mistake to take this text, in which you have obedience in its very highest perfection, as our subject in speaking of the entrance on the course. But it is no mistake. The secret of success in a race is to have the goal clearly defined and aimed at from the very outset.

"He . . . became obedient unto death." There is no other Christ for any of us, no other obedience that pleases God, no other example for us to copy, no other teacher from whom to learn to obey. Christians suffer inconceivably because they do not at once and heartily accept this as the only obedience at which they are to aim. The youngest Christian will find it a strength in the school of Christ to make nothing less from the beginning his prayer and his vow: obedient unto death. It is at once the beauty and the glory of Christ. A share in it is the highest blessing He has to give. The desire for and the surrender to it are possible to the youngest believer.

If you want to be reminded of what it means, think of the story in ancient history. A proud king, with a great army following him, demands the submission of the king of a small but brave nation. When the ambassadors have delivered their message, the second king calls one of his soldiers to stab himself. At once he does it. A second is called; he too obeys at once. A third is summoned; he too is obedient to death.

"Go and tell your master that I have 3,000 such men; let him come."

The king dared count on men who held their lives not dear to them when the king's word called for it.

It is such obedience God wants. It is such obedience Christ gave. It is such obedience He teaches. Be it such obedience and nothing less that we seek to learn. From the very outset of the Christian life let this be our aim: that we may avoid the fatal mistake of calling Christ Master and yet not do what He says.

Let all who have in any degree been convicted of the sin of disobedience listen as we study from God's Word the way to escape from that and to gain access to the life Christ can give—the entrance into the life of full obedience.

## Confession and Cleansing

It is easy to see that this must be the first step. In Jeremiah, the prophetic book which more than any other speaks of the disobedience of God's people, God says, " 'Return, thou backsliding Israel,' saith the Lord . . . 'for I am merciful. . . . Only acknowledge thine iniquity, that . . . ye have not obeyed My voice,' saith the Lord. 'Turn, O backsliding children,' saith the Lord" (Jer. 3:12-14).

Just as there cannot be pardon at conversion without confession, after conversion there cannot be deliverance from the overcoming power of sin and the disobedience it brings, without a new and deeper conviction and confession.

The thought of our disobedience must not be a vague generality. The special things in which we actually disobey must be definitely found out and, in confession, given up and placed in the hands of Christ, and by Him cleansed away. Only then can there be the hope of entering into the way of true obedience.

Let us search our lives by the light of our Lord's teaching.

● Christ appealed to the Law. He was not come to destroy the Law, but to secure its fulfillment. To the young ruler, He said, "Thou knowest the commandments" (Mark 10:19). Let the Law be our first test.

Let us take a single sin such as lying. I had a note from a young lady once, saying that she wished to obey fully and that she felt urged to confess an untruth she had told me. It was not a matter of importance, and yet she rightly judged that the confession would help her cast it from her.

How much there is in ordinary society, how much in school life too that will not stand the test of strict truthfulness! And there are other commandments, up to the very last—with its condemnation of all coveting and lusting after what is not ours—in which too frequently the Christian gives way to disobedience.

All this must come to a complete end. We must confess it and, in God's strength, put it away forever if there is to be any thought of our entering a life of full obedience.
• Christ revealed the new law of love. To be merciful as the Father in heaven, to forgive just as He does, to love enemies and to do good to them that hate us, and to live lives of self-sacrifice and beneficence—this was the religion Jesus taught on earth.

Let us consider an unforgiving spirit when we are provoked or ill-used, unloving thoughts and sharp or unkind words, the neglect of the call to show mercy and do good and bless, all as so much disobedience which must be felt and mourned over and plucked out like a right eye before the power of a full obedience can be ours.
• Christ spoke much of self-denial. Self is the root of all lack of love and obedience. Our Lord called each of His disciples to deny himself, to take up his cross, to forsake all, to hate and to lose his own life, to humble himself and become the servant of all. He did so because self—self-will, self-pleasing, self-seeking—is simply the source of all sin.

When we pander to the flesh by overindulgence in eating and drinking, when we gratify self by seeking or accepting or rejoicing in what indulges our pride, when self-will is allowed to assert itself and we make provision for the fulfillment of its desire, we are guilty of disobedience to His command. This gradually clouds the soul and makes the full enjoyment of His light and peace an impossibility.

● Christ claimed for God the love of the whole heart. For Himself He equally claimed the sacrifice of all to come and follow Him. The Christian who has not definitely within his heart made this his aim, who has not determined to seek for grace in order to live, is guilty of disobedience. There may be much in his religion that appears good and earnest, but he cannot possibly have the joyful consciousness of knowing that he is doing the will of his Lord and keeping His commandments.

When the call is heard to come and now begin anew a true life of obedience, there are many who feel the desire to do so and try quietly to slip into it. They think that by more prayer and Bible study they will grow into it and that it will gradually come. They are greatly mistaken. The word God uses in Jeremiah might teach them their mistake: "Turn, ye backsliding children" (Jer. 3:22).

A soul that is in full earnest and has taken the vow of full obedience may grow out of a feeble obedience into a fuller one. But there is no growing out of disobedience into obedience. A turning back, a turning away, a decision, a crisis is needed. And that only comes by very definite insight into what has been wrong, and its confession with shame and penitence. Then alone will the soul seek for that divine and mighty cleansing from all its filthiness which prepares for the consciousness of the gift of the new heart, and God's Spirit in it causing us to walk in His statutes.

If you would hope to lead a different life, to become a man or a woman of a Christlike obedience unto death, begin by beseeching God for the Holy Spirit of conviction to show you all your disobedience and to lead you in humble confession to the cleansing God has provided. Rest not till you have received it.

### Faith That Obedience Is Possible

This is the second step. To take it we must try and understand clearly what obedience is.

● To this end we must attend carefully to the difference between *voluntary* and *involuntary* sin. It is with the former alone that obedience deals.

We know that the new heart which God gives His child is placed in the midst of the flesh with its sinfulness. Out of this there often arise, even in one who is walking in true obedience, evil suggestions of pride, unlovingness, and impurities, over which he has no direct control. They are in their nature utterly sinful and vile, but they are not imputed to a man as acts of transgression. They are not acts of disobedience which he can break off and cast out as he can the disobedience of which we have spoken. The deliverance from them comes in another way, not through the will of the regenerate man, by which obedience always comes, but through the cleansing power of the blood and the indwelling Christ. As the sinful nature rises, all he can do is to abhor it and trust in the blood that at once cleanses him and keeps him clean.

It is of great consequence to note the distinction. It keeps the Christian from thinking obedience impossible. It encourages him to seek and offer his obedience in the sphere where it can avail. And in the same proportion that the power of the will for obedience is maintained, the power of the Spirit can be trusted and obtained to do the

cleansing work in what is beyond the reach of the will.
● When this difficulty has been removed, often a second
one arises to make us doubt whether obedience is indeed
possible.

Men connect it with the idea of absolute perfection.
They put together all the commands of the Bible, they
think of all the graces these commands point to in their
highest possible measure, and they think of a man with
all those graces, every moment in their full perfection, as
an obedient man. How different is the demand of the
Father in heaven! He takes account of the different powers and attainments of each child of His. He asks of him
only the obedience of each day, or rather, each hour at a
time. He sees whether His child has indeed chosen and
given himself up to the wholehearted performance of
every known command. He sees whether His child is
really longing and learning to know and do all His will.
And when His child does this in simple faith and love, the
obedience is acceptable. The Spirit gives us the sweet
assurance that we are well-pleasing to Him and enables us
to "have . . . confidence toward God . . . because [we
know that] we keep His commandments, and do those
things that are pleasing in His sight" (1 John 3:21-22). This
obedience is indeed an attainable degree of grace. The
faith that it is truly attainable is indispensable to the
obedient walk.

You ask for the ground of that faith in God's Word? You
find it in God's New Covenant promise, "I will . . .
write . . . [My law] in their hearts. I will put My fear in
their hearts, that they shall not depart from Me" (Jer.
31:33; 32:40).

The great defect of the Old Covenant was that it demanded but did not provide the power for obedience. The New Covenant does. The heart means the love, the life. The law put into, written into the heart, means that it has taken possession of the inmost life and love of the renewed man. The new heart delights in the law of God; it is willing and able to obey it.

You doubt this; your experience does not confirm it. No wonder! A promise of God is a thing of faith; you do not believe it and so cannot experience it.

You know what invisible writing fluid is. You write with it on paper, and nothing can be seen by a man who is not in on the secret. Tell him of it, and by faith he knows it. Hold it up to the sun or put some chemical on it, and the secret writing appears. Similarly is God's law written in your heart. Hold up your heart to the light and heat of the Holy Spirit, and you will find this fact to be true. The law written in the heart will mean to you the fervent love of God's commands, with the power to obey them.

How plain, how certain, how all-sufficient the provision is that has been made in the New Covenant, the covenant of grace, for securing our obedience!

A story is told of one of Napoleon's soldiers wounded in battle. The doctor was seeking to extract a bullet that had lodged in the region of the heart, when the soldier cried, "Cut deeper, you will find Napoleon graven there."

Christian, believe that the law lives in your inmost being! Speak in faith the words of David and of Christ: "I delight to do Thy will, O my God: yea, Thy law is within [written on] my heart" (Ps. 40:8).

The faith of this will assure you that obedience is possible. Such faith will help you into the life of true obedience.

## The Step Out of Disobedience

"Return [to Me], ye backsliding children, and I will heal your backslidings" (Jer. 3:22), God said to Israel. They were His people but had turned from Him; the return must be immediate and entire. To turn our backs on the divided life of disobedience and in the faith of God's grace to say, "I will obey," may be the work of a moment.

The power for it, to take the vow and to maintain it, comes from the living Christ. We have said before that the power of obedience lies in the mighty influence of a living personal presence. As long as we took our knowledge of God's will from a book or from men, we could only fail. If we take Jesus in His unchanging nearness as at once our Lord and our strength, we can obey. The voice that commands is the voice that inspires. The eye that guides is the eye that encourages. Christ becomes all in all to us—the Master who commands, the Example who teaches, the Helper who strengthens. Turn from your life of disobedience to Christ; give up yourself to Him in surrender and faith.

In surrender. Let Him have all. Give up your life to be as full of Him, of His presence, of His will, of His service as He can make it. Give up yourself to Him, not to be saved from disobedience so that now you may be happy and live your own life without sinning and trouble. No, but that He may have you wholly for Himself as a vessel and as a channel which He can fill with Himself, with life and love for men in His blessed service.

In faith too. In a new faith. When a soul sees this new thing in Christ, the power for continual obedience, it needs a new faith to take in the special blessing of His great redemption. The faith that only understood that "He . . . became obedient unto death" of His atonement, as a motive to love and obedience, now learns to take the word as Scripture speaks it, "Have this mind in you, which was also in Christ Jesus: who . . . humbled Himself, becoming obedient even unto death" (Phil. 2:5-8, ASV). It believes that Christ has put His own mind and Spirit into us and, in the faith of that, prepares to live and act it out.

God sent Christ into the world to restore obedience to its place in our hearts and lives, to restore man to His place in the obedience to God. Christ came and, becoming obedient unto death, proved what the only true obedience is. He lived it out and perfected it in Himself as a life that He won through death and now communicates to us. The Christ who loves us, who leads and teaches and strengthens us, who lives in us, is the Christ who was obedient unto death. "Obedient unto death" is the very essence of the life He imparts. Shall we not accept it and trust Him to manifest it in us?

Would you enter into the blessed life of obedience? See here the open gate: Christ says, "I am the door" (John 10:7). See here the new and living way: Christ says, "I am the way" (14:6).

We begin to see it; all our disobedience was because we did not know Christ aright. We see it; obedience is only possible in a life of unceasing fellowship with Him. The inspiration of His voice, the light of His eyes, the grasp of His hand make it possible, make it certain.

Come and let us bow down and yield ourselves to this Christ, obedient unto death in the faith that He makes us partakers with Himself of all He is and has.

# CHAPTER SIX

# THE OBEDIENCE OF FAITH

"By faith Abraham . . . obeyed." (Hebrews 11:8)

"By faith Abraham, when he was called to go out into a place which he should after receive for an inheritance, obeyed; and he went out, not knowing whither he went" (Heb. 11:8). He believed that there was a land of Canaan of which God had spoken. He believed in it as a "land of promise" secured to him as an inheritance. He believed that God would bring him there, would show it to him, and give it to him. In that faith he dared go out, "not knowing whither he went." In the blessed ignorance of faith, he trusted God and obeyed, and he received the inheritance.

The land of promise that has been set before us is the blessed life of obedience. We have heard God's call to go out and dwell there; about that there can be no mistake. We have heard the promise of Christ to bring us there and to give us possession of the land; that too is clear and sure. We have surrendered ourselves to our Lord and asked of our Father to make all this true in us. Our desire now is that all our life and work in it may be lifted up to the level of a holy and joyful obedience, and that through us God may make obedience the keynote of the Christian life we aim at promoting in others. Our aim is high; we can only reach it by a new inflow of the power that comes from above. It is only by a faith that gets a new vision and hold of the powers of the heavenly world, secured to us in Christ, that we can obey and obtain the promise.

As we think of all this, of cultivating in ourselves and others the conviction that we only live to please Him and to serve His purposes, some are ready to say: "This is not a land of promise we are called to enter, but a life of burden and difficulty and certain failure."

Do not say so, fellow Christian! God calls you indeed to a land of promise. Come and prove what He can work in you. Come and experience what the nobility is of a Christ-like obedience unto death. Come and see what blessing God will give to him who, with Christ, gives himself wholly to the will of God. Only believe in the glory of this good land of wholehearted obedience and in God who calls you to it, in Christ who will bring you in, in the Holy Spirit who dwells and works all there. He that believes shall enter in.

I wish, then, to speak of the obedience of faith, and of faith as the sufficient power for all obedience. Five simple statements express the disposition of a believing heart, who enters into that life in the good land: (1) I see it, (2) I desire it, (3) I expect it, (4) I accept it, (5) I trust Christ for it.

### Faith Sees It

We have been trying to show you the map of the land and to indicate the most important places in the land, the points at which God meets and blesses the soul. What we need now is in faith to settle the question quietly and definitely. Is there really such a land of promise in which continuous obedience is certainly and divinely possible?

As long as there is any doubt on this point, it is out of the question to go up and possess the land. Just think of Abraham's faith. It rested in God, in His omnipotence and His faithfulness. We have put before you the promises of God. Hear another of them: "A new heart also will I give you. . . . And I will put My Spirit within you, and cause you to walk in My . . . judgments, and [ye shall] do [keep] them" (Ezek. 36:26-27). Here is God's covenant promise. He adds, "I the Lord have spoken it, and I will do it" (v. 36). He undertakes to cause and enable you to obey. In Christ and the Holy Spirit He has made the most wonderful provision for fulfilling His promise.

Just do what Abraham did: fix your heart on God. "He . . . was strong in faith, giving glory to God . . . being fully persuaded that, what He had promised, He was able also to perform" (Rom. 4:20-21). God's omnipotence was Abraham's support. Let it be yours. Look on all the promises God's Word gives of a clean heart, of a heart established blameless in holiness, of a life in righteousness and holiness, of a walk in all the commandments of the Lord unblamable and well-pleasing to Him, of God's working in us to will and to do, of His working in us that which is well-pleasing in His sight, in the simple faith that God says this, and His power can do it. Let the assurance possess you that a life of full obedience is possible. Gaze on the vision until your heart says: "It must be true. It is true. There is a life promised I have never yet known."

### Faith Desires It

When I read the Gospel story and see how ready the sick, the blind, and the needy were to believe Christ's word, I often ask myself what it was that made them so much more ready to believe than we are. The answer I get in the Word is this: that one great difference lies in the honesty and intensity of the desire. They did indeed desire deliverance with their whole hearts. There was no need of pleading with them to make them willing to take His blessing.

Alas, that it should be so different with us! All indeed wish, in a sort of way, to be better than they are. But how few there are who really "hunger and thirst after righteousness"; how few intensely long and cry after a life of close obedience and the continual consciousness of being pleasing to God.

There can be no strong faith without strong desire. Desire is the great motivational power in the universe. It was God's desire to save us that moved Him to send His Son. It is desire that moves men to study and work and suffer. It is the desire alone for salvation that brings a sinner to Christ. It is the desire for God and the closest possible fellowship with Him, that desire to be just what He would have us be and to have as much of His will as possible, that will make the Promised Land attractive to us. It is this which will make us forsake everything to get our full share in the obedience of Christ.

And how can the desire be awakened? Shame on us that we need to ask the question, that the most desirable of all things, likeness to God in the union with His will and doing it, has so little attraction for us! Let us take it as a sign of our blindness and dullness, and beseech God to give us by His Spirit enlightened eyes of the heart, that we may see and know "the riches of the glory of His inheritance" (Eph. 1:18), waiting ahead in the life of true obedience. Let us turn and gaze, in this light of God's Spirit, and gaze again on the life as possible, as certain, as divinely secured and divinely blessed, until our faith begins to burn with desire, and to say, "I do long to have it. With my whole heart I will seek it."

### Faith Expects It

The difference between desire and expectation is great. There is often a strong desire after salvation in a soul who has little hope of really obtaining it. It is a great step forward when desire passes into expectation, and the soul begins to say of spiritual blessing: "I am sure it is for me, and, though I do not see how, I confidently expect to obtain it."

The life of obedience is no longer an unattainable ideal held out by God to make us strive at least to get a little nearer it, but it is a reality meant for the life in flesh and blood here on earth. Expect it as most certainly meant for you. Expect God to make it true.

There is much indeed to hinder this expectation: your past failure, your unfavorable temperament or circumstances, your feeble faith, your difficulty as to what such a devotion—obedient unto death—may demand, your conscious lack of power for it. All this makes you say, "It may be for others; I'm afraid it is not for me." Don't speak that way. You are leaving God out of the picture. Expect it. Begin to say, "It is for me."

Noted German hymnwriter Gerhard Tersteegen had from his youth sought to serve the Lord. After a time the sense of God's grace was withdrawn from him, and for five long years he was as one far away on the great sea, where neither sun nor stars appear. "But my hope was in Jesus." All at once a light broke on him that never went out, and he wrote, with blood drawn from his veins, that letter to the Lord Jesus in which he said: "From this evening to all eternity, Thy will, not mine be done. Command and rule and reign in me. I yield up myself without reserve, and I promise, with Thy help and power, rather to give up the last drop of my blood than knowingly or willingly be untrue or disobedient to Thee." That was his obedience unto death.

Set your heart on obedience and expect it. The same God lives still. Set your hope on Him; He will do it.

## Faith Accepts It

To accept is more than to expect. Many wait and hope and never possess because they do not accept.

To all who have not accepted, and feel as if they were not ready to accept, we say, "Expect." If the expectation be from the heart and be set indeed on God Himself, it will lead the soul to accept. To all who say they do expect, we urgently say, "Accept." Faith has the wondrous God-given power of saying, "I accept, I take, I have."

It is because of the lack of this definite faith, that claims and appropriates the spiritual blessing we desire, that so many prayers appear to be fruitless. For such an act of faith all are not ready. Where there is no true conviction of the sin of disobedience, and, alas, no true sorrow for it; where there is no strong longing or purpose to really obey God in everything; where there is no deep interest in the message of Holy Scripture that God wants to "perfect [us] . . . to do His will" by Himself "working in [us] that which is well pleasing in His sight" (Heb. 13:21), there is no spiritual capacity to accept the blessing. Such a Christian is content to be a babe. He wants only to suck the milk of consolation. He is not able to bear the strong meat which Jesus ate, doing the will of His Father.

And yet the Lord comes to all with the entreaty, "Accept the grace for this wondrous new life of obedience; accept it now." Without this, your act of consecration will come to little. Without this, your purpose to try and be more obedient must fail. Has not God shown you that there is an entirely new position for you to take, a possible position of simple childlike obedience, day by day, to every command His voice speaks to you through the Spirit, a possible position of simple childlike dependence on and experience of His all-sufficient grace, day by day, for every command He gives?

I pray you, even now, take that position, make that surrender, take that grace. Accept and enter on the true life of faith and the unceasing obedience of faith. May your faith be as unlimited and as sure as God's promise and power. As unlimited as your faith is, will your simple childlike obedience be. Oh, ask God for His aid, and accept all He has offered you.

### Faith Trusts Christ for All

"All the promises of God [are] in . . . [Christ Jesus]
. . . and in Him Amen, unto the glory of God by us"
(2 Cor. 1:20). It is possible that as we have spoken of the
life of obedience there have been questions and difficulties rising which you cannot easily answer. You may feel
as if you cannot take it all in at once, or reconcile it with all
the old habits of thought and speech and action. You fear
you will not be able to bring all into subjection at once to
this supreme all-controlling principle: *Do everything as the
will of God; do all as obedience to Him.*

To all these questions there is one answer, one deliverance from all these fears. Jesus Christ, the living Saviour,
knows all, and asks you to entrust yourself to Him for the
wisdom and the power to walk always in the obedience of
faith.

We have seen more than once how His whole redemption, as He effected it, is nothing but obedience. As He
communicates it, it is still the same. He gives us the spirit
of obedience as the spirit of life. This spirit comes to us
each moment through Him. He Himself keeps charge of
our obedience. There is none under heaven but what He
has and gives and works. He offers Himself to us as
surety for its maintenance, and asks us to trust Him for it.
It is in Jesus Himself that all our fears are removed, all our
needs supplied, all our desires met. As He the Righteous
One is your righteousness, He the obedient One is your
obedience.

Will you not trust Him for it? What faith sees and
desires and expects and accepts, surely it dare trust Christ
to give and to work.

72

Will you not take the opportunity today of giving glory to God and His Son by trusting Jesus now to lead you into the Promised Land? Look up to your glorified Lord in heaven and, in His strength, renew with new meaning your vow of allegiance, your vow never to do anything knowingly or willingly that would offend Him. Trust Him for the faith to make the vow, for the heart to keep it, for the strength to carry it out. Trust Him, the living One, by His living presence, to secure both your faith and obedience. Trust Him and venture to join in an act of consecration, in the assurance that He undertakes to be its yes and Amen, to the glory of God by us.

# CHAPTER SEVEN

# THE SCHOOL OF OBEDIENCE: A BASKET OF FRAGMENTS

"Gather up the fragments that remain,
that nothing be lost." (John 6:12)

In this chapter I wish to gather up some points not yet touched on or not expressed with sufficient clearness, in the hope that they may help someone who has indeed enrolled himself in Christ's school of obedience.

## Learning Obedience

First, let me warn against a misunderstanding of the expression "learning obedience." We are apt to think that absolute obedience as a principle—obedience unto death—is a thing that can only be gradually learned. This is a great and most hurtful mistake. What we have to learn, and do learn gradually, is the practice of obedience in new and more difficult commands. But as to the principle, Christ wants us from the very entrance into His school to make the vow of entire obedience.

A little child of five can be as implicitly obedient as a youth of eighteen. The difference between the two lies not in the principle but in the nature of the work demanded.

Though externally Christ's obedience unto death came at the end of His life, the spirit of His obedience was the same from the beginning. Wholehearted obedience is not the end but the beginning of our school life. The end is fitness for God's service when obedience has placed us fully at God's disposal. A heart yielded to God in unreserved obedience is the one condition of progress in Christ's school and of growth in the spiritual knowledge of God's will.

Young Christian, do get this matter settled at once. Remember God's rule: all for all. Give Him all; He will give you all. Consecration avails nothing unless it means presenting yourself as a living sacrifice to do nothing but the will of God. The vow of entire obedience is the entrance fee for him who would be enrolled by no assistant teacher but by Christ Himself in the school of obedience.

## Learning to Know God's Will

This unreserved surrender to obey, as it is the first condition of entering Christ's school, is the only fitness for receiving instruction as to the will of God for us.

There is a general will of God for all His children which we can, in some measure, learn out of the Bible. But there is a special individual application of these commands—God's will concerning each of us personally—which only the Holy Spirit can teach. And He will not teach it except to those who have taken the vow of obedience.

This is the reason why there are so many unanswered

prayers for God to make known His will. Jesus said, "If any man willeth to do His will, he shall know of the teaching, whether it is of God" (John 7:17, ASV). If a man's will is really set on doing God's will, that is, if his heart is given up to do it, and he as a consequence does it as far as he knows it, he shall know what God has further to teach him.

It is simply what is true of every scholar with the art he studies, of every apprentice with his trade, of every man in business—doing is the one condition of truly knowing. And so obedience, the doing of God's will as far as we know it, and the will and the vow to do it all as He reveals it, is the spiritual organ, the capacity for receiving the true knowledge of what is God's will for each of us.

In connection with this let me mention three things.

● Seek to have a deep sense of your very great ignorance of God's will and of your impotence by any effort to know it aright. The consciousness of ignorance lies at the root of true teachableness. "The meek will He guide in . . . His way" (Ps. 25:9), that is, those who humbly confess their need of teaching. Head knowledge only gives human thoughts without power. God by His Spirit gives a living knowledge that enters the love of the heart and works effectually.

● Cultivate a strong faith that God will make you know wisdom in the hidden part, in the heart. You may have known so little of this in your Christian life that the thought appears strange. Learn that God's working, the place where He gives His life and light, is in the heart, deeper than all our thoughts. Any uncertainty about God's will makes a joyful obedience impossible. Believe most confidently that the Father is willing to make known what He wants you to do. Count on Him for this. Expect it with certainty.

● In view of the darkness and deceitfulness of the flesh and fleshly mind, ask God very earnestly for the searching and convincing light of the Holy Spirit. There may be many things which you have been accustomed to think lawful or allowable which your Father wants different. To consider it settled that they are the will of God because you and others think so may effectually shut you out from knowing God's will in other things. Bring everything without reservation to the judgment of the Word, explained and applied by the Holy Spirit. Wait on God to lead you to know that everything you are and do is pleasing in His sight.

## Obedience Unto Death

There is one of the deeper and more spiritual aspects of this truth to which I have not alluded. It is something that as a rule does not come up in the early stages of the Christian life, and yet it is necessary for every believer to know the privileges that await him. There is an experience into which wholehearted obedience will bring the believer, in which he will know that, as surely as with his Lord, obedience leads to death.

Let us see what this means. During our Lord's life, His resistance to sin and the world was perfect and complete. And yet, His final deliverance from their temptations and His victory over their power—achieved by His obedience—was not complete until He had died to the earthly life and to sin. In that death He gave up His life in perfect helplessness into the Father's hands, waiting for Him to raise Him up. It was through death that He received the fullness of His new life and glory. Through death alone, the giving up of the life He had, could obedience lead Him into the glory of God.

The believer shares with Christ in this death to sin. In regeneration he is baptized by the Holy Spirit into it. Because of ignorance and unbelief, he may know little experientially of this entire death to sin. When the Holy Spirit reveals to him what he possesses in Christ and he appropriates it in faith, the Spirit works in him the very same disposition which encouraged Christ in His death. With Christ it was an entire ceasing from His own life, a helpless committal of His Spirit into the Father's hands. This was the complete fulfillment of the Father's command: "Lay down Thy life in My hands." Out of the perfect self-oblivion of the grave He entered the glory of the Father.

It is into this fellowship that a believer is brought. He finds that in the most unreserved obedience for which God's Spirit fits him, there is still a secret element of self and self-will. He longs to be delivered from it. He is taught in God's Word that this can only be by death. The Spirit helps him to claim more fully that he is indeed dead to sin in Christ, and that the power of that death can work mightily in him. He is made willing to be obedient unto death, this entire death to self which makes him truly nothing. In this he finds a full entrance into the life of Christ.

To see the need of this entire death to self, to be made willing for it, to be led into the entire self-emptying and humility of our Lord Jesus—this is the highest lesson that our obedience has to learn. This is, indeed, the Christlike obedience unto death.

There is no room here to enlarge on this. I thought it well to say this much on a lesson which God Himself will, in due time, teach those who are entirely faithful.

### The Voice of Conscience

In regard to the knowledge of God's will, we must see and give conscience its place and submit to its authority.

There are a thousand little things in which the law of nature or education teaches us what is right and good, and in regard to which even earnest Christians do not hold themselves bound to obey. Now, remember, if you are unfaithful in that which is least, who will entrust you with the greater? Not God. If the voice of conscience tells you of some course of action that is the nobler or the better and you choose another because it is easier or pleasing to self, you unfit yourself for the teaching of the Spirit by disobeying the voice of God in nature. A strong will always to do the right, to do the very best as conscience points it out, is a will to do God's will. Paul writes, "I lie not, my conscience also bearing me witness in the Holy Ghost" (Rom. 9:1). The Holy Spirit speaks through conscience. If you disobey and hurt conscience, you make it impossible for God to speak to you.

Obedience to God's will shows itself in tender regard for the voice of conscience. This holds good with regard to eating and drinking, sleeping and resting, spending money and seeking pleasure; let everything be brought into subjection to the will of God.

This leads to another thing of great importance in this connection. If you would live the life of true obedience, see that you maintain a good conscience before God and never knowingly indulge in anything which is contrary to His mind. Conscience is the guardian or monitor God has given you to give warning when anything goes wrong. Up to the light you have, give heed to conscience. Ask God, by the teaching of His will, to give it more light. Seek the witness of conscience that you are acting according to that light. Conscience will become your encouragement and your helper and give you the confidence, both that your obedience is accepted and that your prayer for ever-increasing knowledge of God's will is heard.

### Legal and Evangelical Obedience

Even when the vow of unreserved obedience has been taken, there may still be two sorts of obedience, that of the Law and that of the Gospel. Just as there are two Testaments, an Old and a New, so there are two styles of religion, two ways of serving God. This is what Paul speaks of when he says, "Sin shall not have dominion over you: for ye are not under the Law, but under grace" (Rom. 6:14), and he further speaks of our being "free from the Law" (7:3, ASV), so "that we should serve in newness of spirit, and not in the oldness of the letter" (7:6); and then again reminds us, "Ye received not the spirit of bondage again unto fear; but ye received the spirit of adoption" (8:15, ASV).

The threefold contrast points very evidently to a spiritual danger existing among those Christians still acting as if they were under the Law, serving in the oldness of the

81

letter and in the spirit of bondage. One great cause of the feebleness of so much Christian living is because it is under Law more than under grace. Let us see what the difference is.

What the Law demands from us, grace promises and performs for us. The Law deals with what we ought to do, whether we can or not, and, by the appeal to motives of fear and love, stirs us up to do our utmost. But it gives no real strength and so only leads to failure and condemnation. Grace points to what we cannot do and offers to do it for us and in us.

The Law comes with commands on stone or in a book. Grace comes in a living, gracious Person who gives His presence and His power. The Law promises life if we obey. Grace gives life, even the Holy Spirit, with the assurance that we can obey.

Human nature is ever prone to slip back out of grace into the Law and secretly to trust in trying and doing its utmost. The promises of grace are so divine, the gift of the Holy Spirit to do all in us is so wonderful, that few believe it. This is the reason they never dare take the vow of obedience, or, having taken it, turn back again. I beseech you, study well what Gospel obedience is. The Gospel is Good News. Its obedience is part of that Good News—that grace, by the Holy Spirit, will do all in you. Believe that and let every undertaking to obey be in the joyous hopefulness that comes from faith in the exceeding abundance of grace, in the mighty indwelling of the Holy Spirit, in the blessed love of Jesus whose abiding presence makes obedience possible and certain.

## The Obedience of Love

This is one of the most special and beautiful aspects of Gospel obedience. The grace which promises to work all through the Holy Spirit is the gift of eternal love. The Lord Jesus (who takes charge of our obedience, teaches it, and by His presence secures it to us) is He who loved us unto the death, who loves us with a love that surpasses knowledge. Nothing can receive or know love but a loving heart. And it is this loving heart that enables us to obey. Obedience is the loving response to the divine love resting on us, and it is the only access to a fuller enjoyment of that love.

How our Lord insisted on obedience in His farewell discourse! Three times He repeats it in John 14: "If ye love Me, ye will keep My commandments" (v. 15, ASV); "He that hath My commandments, and keepeth them, he it is that loveth Me" (v. 21); "If a man love Me, he will keep My words" (v. 23). Is it not clear that love alone can give the obedience Jesus asks, and receive the blessing Jesus gives to obedience? The gift of the Spirit, the Father's love and His own, with the manifestation of Himself; the Father's love and His own making their abode with us— loving obedience makes all this possible.

In John 15 Jesus puts it from the other side and shows how obedience leads to the enjoyment of God's love: He kept His Father's commandments and abides in His love. If we keep His commandments, we shall abide in His love. He proved His love by giving His life for us. We are His friends; we shall enjoy His love if we do what He commands us. Between His first love and our love in response to it, between our love and His fuller love in response to ours, obedience is the one indispensable link. True and full obedience is impossible except as we live and love. "This is the love of God, that we keep His commandments" (1 John 5:3).

Beware of a legal obedience, striving after a life of true obedience under a sense of duty. Ask God to show you the "newness of life" which is needed for a new and full obedience. Claim the promise, "[I] will circumcise thine heart . . . to love the Lord thy God with all thine heart . . . and thou shalt return and obey . . . the Lord thy God" (Deut. 30:6-9). Believe in the love of God and the grace of our Lord Jesus. Believe in the Spirit within you, enabling you to love and so causing you to walk in God's statutes. In the strength of this faith, in the assurance of sufficient grace made perfect in weakness, enter into God's love and the life of living obedience it works. For it is nothing but the continual presence of Jesus in His love which can fit you for continual obedience.

### Is Obedience Possible?

I close by once again, and most urgently, pressing home this question. It lies at the very root of life. The secret, half-unconscious thought—that to live always well-pleasing to God is beyond our reach—eats away the very root of our strength. I beseech you to give a definite answer to the question.

If in the light of God's provision for obedience, of His promise of working all His good pleasure in you, of His giving you a new heart, with the indwelling of His Son and Spirit, you still fear obedience is not possible, ask God to open your eyes to truly know His will. If your judgment be convinced and you assent to the truth theoretically and yet fear to give up yourself to such a life, I say to you too: ask God to open your eyes and bring you to know His will for yourself. Beware lest the secret fear of having to give up too much, of having to become too peculiar and entirely devoted to God, keep you back. Beware of seeking just enough religion to ease your conscience and then not desiring to do and be and give God all He is worthy of. And beware, above all, of "limiting" God, of making Him a liar by refusing to believe what He has said He can and will do.

If our study in the school of obedience is to be of any profit, don't rest till you have written this down: *Daily obedience to all that God wills of me is possible, is possible to me. In His strength I yield myself to Him for it.*

But remember, only on one condition. Not in the strength of your resolve or effort, but that the unceasing presence of Christ and the unceasing teaching of the Spirit of all grace and power be your portion. Christ, the obedient One, living in you, will secure your obedience. Obedience will be to you a life of love and joy in His fellowship.

# CHAPTER EIGHT

# OBEDIENCE TO THE LAST COMMAND

"Go ye therefore, and make disciples of all the nations." (Matthew 28:19, ASV)

"Go ye into all the world, and preach the Gospel to every creature." (Mark 16:15)

"As Thou didst send Me into the world, even so sent I them into the world." (John 17:18, ASV)

"Ye shall receive power, when the Holy Spirit is come upon you: and ye shall be My witnesses . . . unto the uttermost part of the earth." (Acts 1:8, ASV)

All these words breathe nothing less than the spirit of world conquest: "all the nations," "all the world," "every creature," "the uttermost part of the earth." Each expression indicates that the heart of Christ was set on claiming His rightful dominion over the world He had redeemed and won for Himself. He counts on His disciples to undertake and carry out the work. As He stands at the foot of the throne, ready to ascend and reign, He tells them, "All authority has been given unto Me in heaven and on earth" (Matt. 28:18, ASV), and points them at once to "all the world," to "the uttermost part of the earth" (Acts 1:8, ASV), as the object of His and their desire and efforts. As the King on the throne, He Himself will be their Helper: "I am with you alway" (Matt. 28:20). They are to be the advance guard of His conquering hosts, even unto the end of the world. He

Himself will carry on the war. He seeks to inspire them with His own assurance of victory, with His own purpose to make this the only thing to be thought of as worth living or dying for—the winning back of the world to its God.

Christ does not teach or argue, ask or plead; He simply commands. He has trained His disciples to obedience. He has attached them to Himself in a love that can obey. He has already breathed His own resurrection Spirit into them. He can count on them. He dares to say to them: "Go ye into all the world." Formerly, during His life on earth, they had more than once expressed their doubt about the possibility of fulfilling His commands. But here, as quietly and simply as He speaks these divine words, they accept them. And no sooner has He ascended than they go to the appointed place to wait for the equipment of a heavenly power from their Lord in heaven, for the heavenly work of making all the nations His disciples. They accepted the command and passed it on to those who through them believed on His name. And within a generation, simple men, whose names we do not even know, had preached the Gospel in Antioch and Rome and the regions beyond. The command was passed on and taken up into the heart and life, as meant for all ages, as meant for every disciple.

The command is for us too, for each one of us. There is in the church of Christ no privileged clan to which alone belongs the honor, nor any servile clan on which alone rests the duty of carrying the Gospel to every creature. The life Christ imparts is His own life, the spirit He breathes is His very own Spirit, the one disposition He works is His own self-sacrificing love. It lies in the very nature of His salvation that every member of His body, in full and healthy access to Him, feels himself urged to impart what he has received. The command is no arbitrary law from without. It is simply the revelation for our intelligent and voluntary consent of the wonderful truth that we are His body, that we now occupy His place on earth, and that His will and love now carry out through us the work He began, and that now in His stead we live to seek the Father's glory in winning a lost world back to Him.

How terribly the church has failed in obeying the command! How many Christians there are who never knew that there was such a command! Many hear of it but do not earnestly set themselves to obey it! And many seek to obey it in such a way and measure as seem to them fitting and convenient.

We have been studying what obedience is. We have professed to give ourselves up to a wholehearted obedience. Surely we are prepared to gladly listen to anything that can help us to understand and carry out this our Lord's last and great command: the Gospel to every creature.

Let me give you what I have to say under the three simple headings: Accept His command. Place yourself entirely at His disposal. Begin at once to live for His kingdom.

## Accept His Command

There are various things that weaken the force of this command. There is the impression that a command given to all and general in its nature is not as binding as one that is entirely personal and specific; that if others do not do their part, our share of the blame is comparatively small; that where the difficulties are very great, obedience cannot be an absolute demand; that if we are willing to do our best, this is all that can be asked of us.

Christians, this is not obedience! This is not the spirit in which the first disciples accepted it. This is not the spirit in which we wish to live with our beloved Lord. We want to say—each one of us—if there be no one else, "I, by His grace, will give myself and my life to live for His kingdom." Let me for a moment separate myself from all others and think of my personal relation to Jesus.

I am a member of Christ's body. He expects every member to be at His disposal, to be animated by His Spirit, to live for what He is and does. It is so with my physical body. I carry every member with me day by day in the assurance that I can count on each one to do its part. Our Lord has taken me so truly up into His body that He can ask and expect nothing else from me. And I have so truly yielded myself to Him that there can be no idea of my wanting anything but just to know and do His will.

Or let me take the illustration of the vine and the branches. The branch has just as much only one object for its being as the vine—bearing fruit. If I really am a branch, I am just as much as He was in the world—only and wholly to bring forth fruit, to live and labor for the salvation of men.

Take still another illustration. Christ has bought me with His blood. No slave conquered by force or purchased by money was ever so entirely the property of his master as my soul, redeemed and won by Christ's blood, given up and bound to Him by love, is His property for Him alone to do with it what He pleases. He claims by divine right, working through the Holy Spirit in an infinite power, and I have given a full assent that I live wholly for His kingdom and service. This is my joy and my glory.

There was a time when it was different. There are two ways in which a man can bestow his money or service on another. Long ago there was a slave who by his trade earned much money. All the money came to the master. The master was kind and treated the slave well. At length the slave, from earnings his master had allowed him, was able to purchase his liberty. In course of time the master became impoverished and had to come to his former slave for help. He was not only able but most willing to give it, and he gave liberally, in gratitude for former kindness.

You see at once the difference between the bringing of his money and service when he was a slave, and his gifts when he was free. In the former case he gave all because it and he belonged to the master. In the latter he only gave what he chose.

In which way ought we to give to Christ Jesus? I fear many, many give as if they were free to give whatever they choose, whatever they think they can afford. But the believer who delights to know that he is the bond slave of redeeming love also delights to lay everything he has at his Master's feet, because he belongs to Him.

Have you ever wondered at the fact that the disciples accepted the Great Commission so easily and so heartily? They came fresh from Calvary where they had seen the blood. They had met the risen One, and He had breathed His Spirit into them. During the forty days, "He through the Holy Ghost had given commandments unto the apostles" (Acts 1:2). Jesus was to them Saviour, Master, Friend, and Lord. His word was with divine power; they could not help but to obey. Oh, let us bow at His feet and yield to the Holy Spirit to reveal and assert His mighty claim, and let us unhesitatingly and with the whole heart accept the command as our one life purpose: the Gospel to every creature!

## Place Yourself at His Disposal

The last great command has been so prominently urged in connection with foreign missions that many are inclined exclusively to confine it to them. This is a great mistake. Our Lord's words, "Make disciples of all the nations . . . teaching them to observe all things whatsoever I commanded you" (Matt. 28:19-20, ASV), tell us what our aim is to be, nothing less than to make every man a true disciple, living in holy obedience to all Christ's will.

What a work there is to be done in our Christian churches and our so-called Christian communities before it can be said that the command has been carried out! And what a need that the whole church with every believer in it realize that to do this work is the sole object of its existence! The Gospel brought fully, perseveringly, savingly to every creature: this is the mission, this ought to be the passion, of every redeemed soul. For this alone is the Spirit and likeness and life of Christ formed in you.

If there is one thing that the church needs to preach in the power of the Holy Spirit, it is the absolute and immediate duty of every child of God not only to take some part in this work, as he may think fit or possible, but to give himself to Christ the Master to be guided and used as He would have. And therefore I say to every reader who has taken the vow of full obedience—and dare we count ourselves true Christians if we have not done so?—place yourself at once and wholly at Christ's disposal. As binding as is the first great command on all God's people, "Thou shalt love the Lord thy God, with all thy heart," is this the last great command too: "The Gospel to every creature." Before you know what your work may be, and before you feel any special desire or call or fitness for any work, if you are willing to accept the command, place yourself at His disposal. It is His duty as Master to train and fit and guide and use you. Fear not; come at once and forever out of the selfish religion which puts your own will and comfort first, and gives Christ what you see fit. Let the Master know that He can have you wholly. Enroll yourself at once with Him as a volunteer for His service— whether you serve Him at home or in another land.

### Act on Your Obedience at Once

Whatever your circumstances, it is your privilege to have within reach souls that can be won for God. All around you there are numberless forms of Christian activity which invite your help and offer you theirs. Consider yourself redeemed by Christ for His service, as blessed with His Spirit to give you the very dispositions that were in Himself, and take up, humbly but boldly, your life calling of winning back the world to God. Whether you are led of God to join some of the many agencies already at work or to walk in a more solitary path, remember not to regard the work as that of your church or society or as your own but as the Lord's. Cherish carefully the consciousness of "doing it unto the Lord," of being a servant who is under orders and simply carrying them out; then your work will not, as is so often the case, come between you and your fellowship with Christ but will link you inseparably to Him, His strength, and His approval.

It is so easy to get so engrossed in the human interest there is in our work that its spiritual character, the supernatural power needed for it, the direct working of God in us and through us—all that can fill us with true heavenly joy and hope—is lost from sight. Keep your eye on your Master, on your King, on His throne. Before He gave the command and pointed His servants to the great field of the world, He first drew their eyes to Himself on the throne: "All power is given unto Me in heaven and in earth" (Matt. 28:18). It is the vision, the faith in Christ on the throne, that reminds us of the need and assures us of the sufficiency of His divine power. Obey not a command but the living Almighty Lord of glory; faith in Him will give you heavenly strength.

These words preceded the command, and then there followed, "Lo, I am with you alway." It is not only Christ on the throne—glorious vision!—that we need, but Christ with us here below, in His abiding presence, Himself working for us and through us. Christ's power in heaven, Christ's presence on earth—between these two pillar promises lies the gate through which the church enters to the conquest of the world. Let each of us follow our Leader, receive from Him our orders as to our share in the work, and never falter in the vow of obedience that has given itself to live wholly for His will and His work alone.

Such a beginning will be a training time, preparing us fully to know and follow His leading. If His pleading call for the millions of dying heathen comes to us, we shall be ready to go. If His providence does not permit our going, our devotion at home will be as complete and intense as if we had gone. Whether it be at home or abroad, if only the ranks of the obedient, the servants of obedience, the obedient unto death, are filled up, Christ shall have His heart's desire, and His glorious thought—the Gospel to every creature—will find its accomplishment!

Blessed Son of God! Here I am. By Thy grace, I give my life to carrying out Thy last great command. Let my heart be as Thy heart. Let my weakness be as Thy strength. In Thy name I take the vow of entire and everlasting obedience. Amen.

# ABSOLUTE SURRENDER*

"And Ben-hadad the king of Syria gathered all his host together: and there were thirty and two kings with him, and horses, and chariots: and he went up and besieged Samaria, and warred against it. And he sent messengers to Ahab king of Israel into the city, and said unto him, 'Thus saith Ben-hadad, "Thy silver and thy gold is mine; thy wives also and thy children, even the goodliest, are mine.' " And the king of Israel answered and said, 'My Lord, O king, according to thy saying, I am thine, and all that I have.' " (1 Kings 20:1-4)

Wh5at Ben-hadad asked was *absolute surrender;* and what Ahab gave was what was asked of him—*absolute surrender.* I want to use these words: "My lord, O king, according to thy saying, I am thine, and all that I have," as the words of absolute surrender, with which every child of God ought to yield himself to his Father. We have heard it already, but we need to hear it very definitely—the condition of God's blessing is absolute surrender of all into His hands. If our hearts are willing for that, there is no end to what God will do for us, and to the blessing He will bestow.

*Absolute surrender*—let me tell you where I discovered

*A chapter from Andrew Murray's devotional classic of the same name, first published in 1895.

this term of obedience. I have often used it and you may be familiar with it. But recently in Scotland, I was with a group of Christian workers talking about the condition of Christ's church, and what the great need of the church and of believers is. There was in our group a godly worker involved in a training ministry and I asked him what he thought was the great need of the church and the message that ought to be preached. He answered very quietly and simply and determinedly: *"Absolute surrender to God is the one thing."* The words struck me as never before. And that man began to tell how he finds that if his workers are sound on that point, even though they sometimes go backward, they are willing to be taught and helped, and they always improve; whereas, others who are not committed to full surrender very often go backward spiritually and leave the work. The condition for obtaining God's full blessing is *absolute surrender* to Him.

Your God in heaven answers the prayers which you have offered for blessing on yourselves, and for blessing around you, by this one demand: *Are you willing to surrender yourself absolutely into His hands?* There are hundreds of hearts who have answered yes, and there are hundreds more who long to say yes but hardly dare to do so. And there are hearts who have said yes, but who have yet miserably failed, and who feel themselves condemned because they did not find the secret of the power to live that life. May God have a word for us all!

## God Claims Our Surrender

Let me say, first of all, *God claims surrender from us.* Yes, it has its foundation in the very nature of God. God cannot do otherwise. Who is God? He is the fountain of life, the only source of existence and power and goodness, and throughout the universe there is nothing good but what God works. God has created the sun, the moon, and the stars, the flowers, the trees, and the grass; and are they not all absolutely surrendered to God? Do they not allow God to work in them just what He pleases? When God clothes the lily with its beauty, is it not yielded up, surrendered, given over to God as He works in it its beauty? And God's redeemed children, oh, can you think that God can work His work if there is only half or a part of them surrendered? God cannot do it. God is life, and love, and blessing, and power, and infinite beauty, and God delights to communicate Himself to every child who is prepared to receive Him; but, ah! this lack of absolute surrender is the one thing that hinders God.

You know in daily life what absolute surrender is. You know that everything has to be given up to its special, definite object and service. I have a pen in my pocket, and that pen is absolutely surrendered to the one work of writing, and that pen must be absolutely surrendered to my hand if I am to write properly with it. If another holds it partly, I cannot write properly. This coat is absolutely given up to me to cover my body. A church building is entirely given up to religious services. And now, do you expect that in your immortal being, in the divine nature that you have received by regeneration, God can work His work, every day and every hour, unless you are entirely given up to Him? God cannot. The temple of Solomon was absolutely surrendered to God when it was dedicated to Him. And every one of us is a temple of God, in which

God will dwell and work mightily on one condition—absolute surrender to Him. God claims it, God is worthy of it, and without it God cannot work His blessed work in us.

### God Works Our Surrender

God not only claims surrender, *but God will work it Himself.* I am sure there is many a heart that says: "Ah, but that absolute surrender implies so much!" Some may feel, "Oh, I have passed through so much trial and suffering, and there is so much of the self-life still remaining, and I dare not face giving it up entirely, because I know it will cause so much trouble and agony." Alas! alas! that God's children have such thoughts of Him, such cruel thoughts. God does not ask you to give the perfect surrender in *your* strength, or by the power of *your* will; God is willing to work it in you. Do we not read, "It is God that works in you both to will and to do of His good pleasure"? (Phil. 2:13)

Look at the men in the Old Testament, like Abraham. Do you think it was by accident that the Lord found the father of the faithful and the friend of God? Do you think it was Abraham himself, apart from God, who had such remarkable faith and obedience and devotion? You know it is not so. God raised him up, and prepared him as an instrument for His glory. Did not God say to Pharaoh, "For this cause have I raised thee up, for to show in thee My power"? (Ex. 9:16) And if God said that of him, will not God say it far more of every child of His? Oh, I want to encourage you, and I want you to cast away every fear. Come with that feeble desire; and if there is the fear, "My desire is not strong enough, I am not willing for every-thing that may come, I do not feel bold enough to say I can conquer everything"—I pray you, learn to know and trust your God. Say: "My God, I am willing that Thou shouldst make me willing." If there is anything holding you back, or any sacrifice you are afraid of making, come to God and discover how gracious He is, and be not afraid that He will command from you what He will not bestow. God comes and offers to work this absolute surrender in you. All these searchings and hungerings and longings that are in your heart are the drawings of the divine magnet, Christ Jesus, who lived a life of absolute surren-der. He has possession of you, He is living in your heart by His Holy Spirit. Don't hinder Him anymore. Trust Him fully.

## God Accepts Our Surrender

The third thought. God not only claims surrender and works it, but *God accepts it when we bring it to Him*. God works it in the secret of our hearts, God urges us by the hidden power of His Holy Spirit to come and speak it out, and we have to bring and to yield to Him that absolute surrender. But remember, when you come and bring God that absolute surrender, it may, as far as your feelings or your consciousness go, be a thing of great imperfection, and you may doubt and hesitate and say, "Is it absolute?" But, remember there was once a man to whom Christ had said, "If thou canst believe, all things are possible to him that believeth" (Mark 9:23); and his heart was afraid, and he cried out, "Lord, I believe, help Thou mine unbelief" (v. 24). And that was a faith that triumphed over the devil, and the evil spirit was cast out. And if you come and say, "Lord, I yield myself in absolute surrender to my God," even though it be with a trembling heart and with the consciousness, "I do not feel the power, I do not feel the determination, I do not feel the assurance," it will succeed. Be not afraid, but come just as you are, and even in the midst of your trembling the power of the Holy Spirit will work.

Have you never yet learned the lesson that the Holy Spirit works with mighty power, while on the human side everything appears feeble? Look at the Lord Jesus Christ in Gethsemane. We read that He, "through the eternal Spirit," offered Himself a sacrifice unto God (Heb. 9:14). The almighty Spirit of God was enabling Him to do it. And yet what agony and fear and exceeding sorrow came over Him, and how steadfastly He prayed! Externally you can see no sign of the mighty power of the Spirit, but the Spirit of God was there. And even so, while you are feeble and fighting and trembling, in faith in the hidden work of God's Spirit, do not fear, but yield yourself completely.

When you yield yourself in absolute surrender, let it be in the faith that God indeed accepts it. That is the great point, and that is what we so often miss—that believers should be thus occupied with God in this matter of surrender. I beseech you to be occupied with God. There is a God present who takes note of your act of surrender, and writes it down in His book, and there is a God present who at that very moment takes possession of you. You may not feel it, you may not realize it, but God takes possession if you will trust Him.

102

### God Maintains Our Surrender

A fourth thought. God not only claims surrender, and works it, and accepts it when I bring it, but *God maintains it*. That is the great difficulty with many. People say: "I have consecrated myself to God, but it has passed away. I know it may last for a week or for a month, but away it fades, and after a time it is all gone."

But when God has begun the work of absolute surrender in you, and when God has accepted your surrender, then God holds Himself bound to care for it and to keep it. Will you believe that?

In this matter of surrender there are two parties, *God and I*—I a worm, God the everlasting and omnipotent Jehovah. Worm, will you be afraid to trust yourself to this mighty God? God is willing. Oh, that every one of us might hear His voice asking us, "Believest thou that I can do this, that I can keep thee continually, day by day, and moment by moment?" What have you sung in that beautiful chorus?

Moment by moment I'm *kept* in His love;
Moment by moment I've life from above.

If God allows the sun to shine upon you moment by moment, without intermission, will not God let His life shine upon you every moment? And why have you not experienced it? Because you have not trusted God for it, and you do not surrender yourself absolutely to God in that trust.

A life of absolute surrender has its difficulties. I do not deny that. Indeed, it has something far more than difficulties; it is a life that with men is absolutely impossible. But by the grace of God, by the power of God, by the power of the Holy Spirit dwelling in us, it is a life to which we are destined, and a life that is possible for us, praise God! God will maintain it. Perhaps you've read about George Müller who, on his ninetieth birthday, recalled all God's goodness to him. What did he say he believed to be the secret of his happiness, and of all the blessing which God had given him? He said he believed there were two reasons. One was that he had been enabled by grace to maintain a good conscience before God day by day; the other was that he was a lover of God's Word. A good conscience in unfeigned obedience to God day by day, and fellowship with God every day in His Word and in prayer—that is a life of absolute surrender.

Such a life has two sides—on the one side, *absolute surrender to work what God wants me to do*; on the other side, *to let God work what He wants to do*.

## God's Work and Ours

First, absolute surrender means *doing what God wants me to do*. Give up yourself absolutely to the will of God. You know something of that will; not enough, far from all. So say absolutely to the Lord God: "By Thy grace I desire to do Thy will in everything, every moment of every day." Say: "Lord God, not a word on my tongue but for Thy glory, not a movement of my temper but for Thy glory, not an affection of love or hate in my heart but for Thy glory, and according to Thy blessed will." Someone says, "Do you think that possible?" I ask, "What has God promised you, and what can God do to fill a vessel absolutely surrendered to Him?" God waits to bless us in a way beyond what we expect. From the beginning ear has not heard, neither has the eye seen, what God has prepared for them that wait for Him. God has prepared unheard-of things, things you never can think of; blessings much more wonderful than you can imagine, more mighty than you can conceive. They are divine blessings.

On the other side, absolute surrender means *letting Him work in me to will and to do of His good pleasure*, as He has promised to do. Yes, the living God wants to work in His children in a way that we cannot understand, but that nonetheless God's Word has revealed, and He wants to work in us every moment of the day. God is willing to maintain our lives; only let our absolute surrender be one of simple, childlike, and unbounded trust.

The last thought. This absolute surrender to God *will wonderfully bless us*. What Ahab said to his enemy, King Ben-hadad—"My lord, O king, according to thy word I am thine, and all that I have"—shall we not say to our God and loving Father? If we do say it, God's blessing is ours. God wants you to be separate from the world; you are called to come out from the world that hates God. Come out for God, and say: "Lord, anything for Thee." If you say that with prayer, and speak that into God's ear, He will accept it, and He will teach you what it means.

Can God fill you, can God bless you, if you are not absolutely surrendered to Him? He cannot. Let us believe God has wonderful blessings for us, if we will but stand up for Him, and say, be it with a trembling will, yet with a believing heart: "O God, I accept Thy demands, I am Thine and all that I have. Absolute surrender is what my soul yields to Thee by divine grace."

You may not have such strong and clear feelings of deliverance as you would desire to have, but humble yourselves in His sight, and acknowledge that you have grieved the Holy Spirit by your self-will, self-confidence, and self-effort. Bow humbly before Him in the confession of that, and ask Him to break your heart and to bring you into the dust before Him. Then, as you bow before Him, just accept God's teaching that in your flesh "there dwells no good thing," and that nothing will help you except another Life which must come in. You must deny self once and for all. Denying self must every moment be the power of your life, and then Christ will come in and take possession of you.

When was Peter delivered? When was the change accomplished? The change began with Peter weeping, and the Holy Spirit came down and filled his heart. God the Father loves to give us the power of the Spirit. We have the Spirit of God dwelling within us. We come to God confessing that, and praising God for it; and yet confessing how we have grieved the Spirit. And then we bow our knees to the Father to ask that He would strengthen us with all might by the Spirit in the inner man, and that He would fill us with His mighty power. And as the Spirit reveals Christ to us, Christ comes to live in our hearts forever, and the self-life is cast out.

In that same humiliation we want to confess before God the state of the whole church. No words can tell the sad state of the church of Christ on earth. I wish I had words to speak what I sometimes feel about it. Just think of the Christians around you. I do not speak of nominal Christians, or of professing Christians, but I speak of hundreds and thousands of honest, earnest Christians who are not living a life in the power of God or to His glory. So little power, so little devotion or consecration to God, so little conception of the truth that a Christian is a man utterly surrendered to God's will! Oh, we want to confess the sins of God's people around us, and to humble ourselves. We are members of that sickly body, and the sickliness of the body will hinder us, and break us down, unless we come to God, and in confession separate ourselves from partnership with worldlinesss, with coldness toward each other, unless we give up ourselves to be entirely and wholly for God.

Finally, remember that death was the path to glory for Christ. For the joy set before Him He endured the Cross. The Cross was the birthplace of His everlasting glory. Do you love Christ? Do you long to be *in* Christ, and not *like* Him? Let death be to you the most desirable thing on earth; death to self, and fellowship with Christ. Separation—do you think it a hard thing to be called to be entirely free from the world, and by that separation to be united to God and His love, by separation to become prepared for living and walking with God every day? Surely we should say, "Anything to bring me to separation, to death, for a life of full fellowship with God and Christ." Cast your self-life and flesh-life at the feet of Jesus. Then trust Him. Do not try to understand it all, but come in the living faith that Christ will come into you with the power of His death and the power of His life; and then the Holy Spirit will bring the whole Christ—Christ crucified and Christ risen and living in glory—into your heart.